GAIL BREWER-GIORGIO

IS ELVIS ALIVE?

Tudor Publishing Company
New York and Los Angeles

Dedicated to those special G's; Carm, Jim, Chris, Maria, Amy, Sheila and those tiny g's; beautiful Tasha, little Carm and precious Noel—even April

Aunt Mim always.

And Mom and Dad G. Love and hugs.

PRELUDE

People ask me why I've waited so long to tell what really happened. And there are a number of reasons; moral, financial, that this is not a simple story to tell and that it is ongoing. But enough time has passed. Newspapers, magazines, radio and television stations across the country have discovered my inadvertent role in possibly one of the most elaborate, shocking coverups of this century.

It is my turn to set the facts straight.

Before I begin to unravel this explosive story, it is essential that I establish my own credibility. What has happened to me, both professionally and personally, is serious. It's about freedom of speech, about subtle pay offs and gag orders and it involves a possible revelation so extraordinary that, unless you know who I am and what my background is, you would conclude that what I am about to reveal, borders on lunacy.

I have been a professional journalist, writer and novelist for the past twenty years. My work has appeared in both newspapers and magazines in the United States and Canada. I worked in advertising, country music promotion, video and films.

No work of fiction could have experienced what ORION, my first novel, did.

Most people in America have a keen recollection of where they were and what they were doing on August 16, 1977, the day Elvis Presley "died". And so do I. Although not an avid Elvis fan, I remember when I heard that he had "died," becoming oddly intrigued. Like millions of Americans I couldn't get enough information. I couldn't stop thinking about it. I became obsessed. I put down the novel I had been working on and three days after Elvis's "death" I started writing ORION. I had no choice. The book seemed to "write itself."

Orion would be a combination of Jesus and mythology brought to life through a contemporary hero—a singer who would win a "great prize" and because of his intense talent his life would suffer and he would be in great danger. Orion would possess certain psychic connections, would sing one last time, fake his death and disappear—to Hawaii.

I finished a first draft in 54 days.

From the beginning ORION generated great interest among agents and movie people. By 1979 I had signed with a top New York publishing house. I and ORION were on our way. Suddenly the rug was pulled out from under me. I was told never to mention Elvis Presley in connection with ORION. My publisher stopped returning my phone calls. And ORION mysteriously started to disappear from bookstore shelves all over the country. Too many people were asking too many questions about August 16, 1977—including a question I may have answered via fiction: Did a famous singer hoax his own death?

Bizarre? Ridiculous? Is Elvis still alive? Consider the following:

—a taped conversation thought to be recorded about four years after August 16, 1977 may contain the voice of Elvis Presley. It has been given to a voice print expert. In a later chapter I will discuss this tape, how it was given to me, what it says.

—a taped video of a news program on KCOP television in Los Angeles featuring a picture taken by photographer Mike Joseph four months after the "death" of Elvis Presley. The picture is part of a sequence and authorities have documented that the negatives have not been altered. Mike Joseph captured a face in the door of Elvis's poolhouse, beyond Mediation Gardens. The face looks remarkably like Elvis Presley.

—late night telephone calls and taped conversations . . . some possibly with a voice the world mourns.

In the following pages I will tell you about some of the people who say they have seen Elvis since August 16, 1977.

They are reputable and credible. I'll tell you of at least one place where Elvis is thought to be living. As a writer and a journalist I try to document the largest part of what I am detailing. Some people close to Elvis have requested that certain segments not be attributed to them despite witnesses to their revelations. I try to honor this as much as possible.

For ten years I have deliberately sat on what may be the "biggest story" of the century, but the climate has changed. Something is about to happen. Too much outside my silence is being spoken. Now is the time to tell the world what happened to me, how it began, how I became a victim, while at the same time becoming a hub in a many spoked wheel, how I am, even today, a "David" standing in the shadow of a mighty "Goliath."

A literary agent remarked recently, "I think this is a Musical Watergate."

A Musical Watergate indeed!

THIS STRANGE DAY

That strange day in August 1977, the furthest thing from my mind was cover-ups or mind-boggling events. I had just left a business meeting with the intention of stopping off at the grocery store. I recall how uncomfortable I was in the heat of that late summer afternoon. As soon as I started the car, I switched on the air conditioning and the radio. Slowly I pulled into traffic, my mind working on the novel begun two years earlier, a slow-to-be-finished novel squeezed between writing assignments and a growing family. A jolt speared my lethargic creativity. My body stiffened as my hands squeezed the wheel of the car.

Elvis Presley is dead.

Was that what I just heard the announcer say?
Soft music had been interrupted. "At the age of 42 Elvis Presley has died in Memphis . . ."
A combination of puzzlement, amazement and shock made me want to know more, despite the fact I was not a fan. I owned no Elvis Presley records, had never seen his movies other than television clips, had never been to a concert and possessed only general media information on him. Still, like millions of Americans, I was instantly hooked. An almost macabre-like fascination obsessed me; I wanted as many details as possible. I changed channels; normal broadcasting had been interrupted and, as though one-voice-in-unison, the

announcement was the same: Elvis Presley is dead of a heart attack at age 42 . . .''

Airlines were already reporting a mass exodus toward Memphis. Ordinary, thinking, rational people were loading their children and thrown-together packings into their automobiles and heading in one direction, to stand outside a musical-scaled iron gate.

My astonishment grew. After all, a President had not been assassinated, a country had not toppled. A rock 'n roll singer had died—that's all. Yet this news was capturing the attention of the entire world. Why? As the newscasts continued into the evening with footage showing Elvis' early years, radio stations across the nation played only Elvis music. It was frightening, a phenomenon beyond reason. Even then I was feeling an energy I could not understand and, like everyone else, was caught in that same phenomenon which challenged all reasoning.

Still, reasoning, rational newscasters were involved. David Brinkley, devoting three minutes to Elvis Presley, closed the segment with the news that NBC would present a late-night special on the king, one that would delay The Tonight Show by half an hour. Harry Reasoner announced that ABC would feature a half-hour news special on Elvis following the late evening news. CBS was planning a special on the life of Elvis Presley. Record stores universally reported a sell-out business of millions of Elvis' record albums.

While the world's tears intermingled, a new market of devoted fans were born, and they too, making annual pilgrimages to Memphis, would admire, adore and enshrine a mortal.

He was now more than a king. He was a Musical Messiah.

I had to learn why.

Still, had I known then how bizarre such literary travels would take me, I doubt I would have continued. Doing so could place my personal career and professional integrity up for ridicule. More often than not I deliberately pulled back, deciding that what I was discovering was too unbelievable. But because what occurred happened in increments, I proceeded, often innocent and blind and occasionally ''taken in.''

Now at a distance, since the picture is more complete, can I truly see its incredulity.

A writer's imagination is a strange friend, oftentimes betraying conscious deliberations. I was no different. Nebulous questions were plaguing a curious mind. That night I awoke to pen an "Ode to Elvis," which appeared in THE MARIETTA DAILY JOURNAL a few days later.

Did she rock the baby close and count her blessings and thank God that her son had lived? For only moments before her new son's twin had died and a cold fear must have gripped her heart. But the new babe wriggled and cried and his lungs were strong. Her son, her only child, would indeed live.

And as she continued to caress and marvel at his small mighty wonder, the hopes of all new mothers must have teased her mind and tripped her heart. Would he call her "mama" or "mommy" or "mom"? Would he be as special to the world as he now was to her? Whatever his destiny, she must have silently prayed, "Let him be happy."

She must have felt, like most new mothers feel, a sacred kinship with God and the miracle of birth and her partnership in it. She had given a new child to the world, and she would truly love him. She would love him with the open protectiveness of a free love.

Then Gladys Presley's child grew, and he was beautiful and kind and good. He would sing and imitate and wriggle and dance—and track mud into the house. His dimples would deepen and his half smile widen and he disarmed her mocked anger. Yet I wonder. Did Gladys ever suspect someday this boy-child would be a king? Could she have ever known beforehand that her mortal, feet-of-clay rascal would be godified and idolized and totally imprisoned? If, with this knowledge, would Gladys have given her freedom moving son-of-song to the world, to the world whose love would sever from him even the simplest of mortal freedoms?

Still I wonder? If, after Gladys left, did she too suffer the internal pains that chained her boy, that made him the victim of an adoring mob? Did she so suffer with him in his agony of world withdrawal that in one final act of compassion she called him back?

. . . and "that is that" I thought. I am rid of this craziness forever. I mailed the ode.

How foolish of me to think that I was any different from a world not ready to let go. I went into my kitchen and poured a cup of tea, wanting not to turn on the television or radio, wanting to draw back from the multi-tributes coming in from movie stars, sports figures, fans. President Jimmy Carter said, "His death deprives our country of a part of itself. He was unique and irreplaceable." John Lennon said, "If there hadn't been an Elvis Presley there would have never been any Beatles . . ." Frank Sinatra stopped his show to say, "We lost a good friend today." From all points of the globe came sentiments eulogizing the passing of an entertainer born in the backwoods of Mississippi.

I turned on the television. ". . . record sales have climbed to their highest level in ten years," said one announcer.

"At the age of 42 Elvis' career was all but over. Had he continued in such an overweight and emotionally-drained condition, he would have been reduced to laughing stock," said another. "Death has made Elvis Presley a martyr."

"Elvis was a little Memphis, a little arrogance, a little piety."

". . . but Elvis Presley was ours. And we adored him, adulated him."

To this day I don't know what drove me back to the typewriter. I sent a piece to the editor of an Atlanta newspaper:

Is The King Dead?

We were the new youth of the fifties and you, Elvis, were our wiggling, shaking, shouting messiah. You scorched with explosion and you lit the fuse of our own exploding freedom. You were ours and through you and by you we were also able to shock. You became Elvis while we grew and tried to become—ourselves. You were our Virgin Adventurer, but we were the ones who held the freedom to venture. You gave us courage to be free but in the giving, we took yours. You gifted us with your golden talent and we in turn gilded you, enshrined you and adored you.

—and tragically imprisoned you. While the entire universe was ours to freely roam, yours was the small world

7

which existed behind the confines of a musical scaled iron wall. The world adulated you and loved you and demanded—always—a piece of you. They became a mob. Their adulation became your grief. Their grabbing your enemy. We betrayed you, and perhaps that is why we take your leaving so deeply. No mortal deserves godification during a lifetime. You gave. We took. We stole even the simplest of pleasures.

Were you ever able to wheel your infant baby down the commonest street? Were you ever able to take her innocent hand in yours and show her the miracle of a zoo in the open sunlight? Were you ever able to romp on the white sands of any beach? I doubt it. After all, gods do not seek such mundane freedoms.

Or do they?

We mourn you with the same painful sadness as one mourns lost youth and frenzied innocence. We mourn your now sealed talent, but more we mourn the person we never allowed you to be. For if the king is dead, then we, his disciples, "loved him to death."

Ironically, you once said, "If I can't move, then I am dead."

Yet—is the king really dead?

Jolted again, I questioned why I was writing this—this rambling, sympathetic jargon, this "I-am-sorry-prayer." Still, I sealed the envelope and mailed another piece of writing, hoping this final act would exorcise whatever guilt was inhibiting my creativity.

It was no use. The novel I was earlier working on became a shadow. Strange emotions invaded my mind, and I seemed locked into something—something undefined that needed expression and definition—actually demanded it. I had no choice. The novel ORION began to write itself on the third day after the "death" of Elvis Presley.

Before I looked up what the word "Orion" meant, I knew that Orion was a January constellation and at the same instant knew that my central character would be a combination of Jesus and mythology brought to life through a contemporary hero. I then looked up the mythologial meaning of Orion, and thus my Prologue and Epilogue were born.

THE MYTHOLOGICAL ORION

In the lore of gods and goddesses, Orion was a youth of extraordinary beauty and great stature, a hunter in the universe. During most of his life, he searched in blindness, but ultimately recovered his sight. After he died, he was fixed by the ancients as a heavenly constellation—a giant and brilliant cluster of stars perceived as a hunter whose girdle was made of three stars.

Legend tells of a mortal counterpart named "Arion," who lived about 700 B.C. It is said that he had gone from Corinth to Sicily to take part in a music contest as a master of the lyre. He won the great prize and on his voyage home, sailors planned to kill him for it.

The god Apollo told "Arion" in a dream of his danger, and how to survive. When the sailors attacked "Arion," he begged a final favor: to let him play and sing once more.

At the end of the song, "Arion" threw himself into the sea where dolphins, enchanted by "Arion's" music, bore him safely to shore.

My hero, Orion, would be a singer, would win a "great prize" and would possess psychic attributes. Because of his gifts, his life would suffer and he would be in great danger. He would sing one last time, then fake his own death by going to a distant shore.

I chose Hawaii for Orion's final escape from life. And I wondered, was Elvis' middle name Aron a derivation of the name Arion? Was something beyond my own imaginings at work? Had I tapped into a bizarre truth? I was unable to answer those questions back in August of 1977. Ten years later, after seeing the book mysteriously disappear from bookstores across the nation, having become a victim, having been told never to mention Elvis Presley in connection with ORION by a major publisher who paid me great sums of money, having witnessed firsthand a possible cover-up, I answer "yes." Yes, I may have tapped into *something*.

Perhaps, even though you'll read the whole of ORION, studying the Prologue will help you understand what was happening and better relate to my position.

9

PROLOGUE

At the height of the massive winding staircase the man paused. He looked up, allowing the depth of his weary eyes to explore the dome of the high ceiling, resting on its center. The mural which long ago had been covered with white paint, was now faintly exposed, almost as though it had a life of its own, determined never to be shut away from all that was visible.

How many times had he ordered that ceiling repainted? But the mural persisted in breaking through, teasing him, teasing his patience, his endurance. He could have had it sandblasted into eternity but strangely he had chosen the immortality of the thin, milky covering. He looked down, mentaly traveling each carpeted stair step until his dense lavender eyes settled on the yellow marble foyer.

A statue of Pallas Athena stood in full view. When he had purchased the old Byzantine church years ago and had it renovated into his Nashville home, his Dixie-Land, he had chosen the virgin goddess to adorn his entrance. Athena was an odd contradiction of wisdom and war, but above all she was the supreme patroness of the arts. Only lately, when introspection preoccupied his thoughts, had he suspected it was the strain of his mother's premature death which had prompted Athena's purchase. His pulse quickened angrily. Athena was a lifeless statue, dammit! Nothing more than a hideous hallucination of a demented mind! Virgins and goddesses, damn kings and legends!

10

Slowly he began the deep descent, each step hesitant. His right hand trembled and he grabbed the banister. An involuntary shudder vibrated through him. Today was the day: freedom. After 20 incredible years of incarceration his day had come, a day he doubted could materialize, but one which nevertheless had sustained his existence.

He heard a sharp click as his boot-heel met with the hard marble floor. He paused. Above him dangled a revolving ball of pieces of colored glass and mirrors which, turning, became a kaleidoscope of colors.

Danielle hated that ornament. "It belongs at a high school prom, Orion, not here! What on earth prompted you to install such a monstrosity?" She said it was "tacky" and "immature."

The thought of Danielle filled him with a kaleidoscope of colors, all warm—his Danielle, but not his. Never again.

As the mirrored ball revolved above him, a flash of memories swam through him, spinning him in a caecum where it seemed even the depth of his bowels spilled downward. Dear Jesus! When would the agony of memory end?

The library was at the far end of the foyer; its thickly carved rosewood doors were closed. His breath caught. Mac Weiman would be sitting behind the desk he used whenever he visited Dixie-Land. Although the man was in his sixties, the years had done little to diminish his enormous physical bearing. Danielle once told Orion she was afraid of the man, and although Orion called her foolish, he understood her feelings. Usually Mac would be seated, his legs crossed, on the large scarred desk. The black leather swivel chair would be tilted. Mac's scrutinizing black eyes would be half closed and he would be chewing that damned cigar.

Orion Eckley Darnell's mouth cornered into the famous smile as he shook his head. Even though he was outside the closed library doors he could smell the stale, heavy odor of Mac's cheap cigar. The man was amazing: After all the millions he had stashed away he was still the cheapest s.o.b. Orion knew.

The gold-leaf mirror on the wall beside Orion caught his attention, and for a moment he was mesmerized by the stranger he saw. There was little in the mirror that resembled the man he had been or the man Mac had created. The image staring at Orion was not the man God created, but another

11

form molded ingeniously by the musically messianic Mac Weiman.

The truth would be revealed soon. Opening the wide doors to the library, Orion walked in. Mac was seated behind the desk, but not in his usual position. Both feet were planted on the floor, and he was leaning forward, his hands folded in front of him. His gray and balding head was lowered, and if Orion did not know better he would have thought the ageless man was praying. Quietly Orion locked the doors as he stared silently at Mac.

Mac raised his eyes and Orion thought for one startling moment the man had been crying. Crying? Jesus Christ! Mac was the hardest, cruelest wheeler-dealer ever to hit Nashville or the entire South, so what could bring such a bullheaded man to tears? During that one second, Orion's eyes locked with those of the man who controlled his life. In that second, Orion knew.

Orion nodded in understanding. "Now?" he asked.

Mac rose slowly. "Yes. Now."

Following Mac to a shadowed corner of the library, Orion gasped aloud. On a white marble bench rested a coffin. Mac half pushed, half led Orion toward it. The closer they came, the more ominous appeared the death-box. Stopping in front of it, Mac clenched Orion's cold, trembling hand, then slowly lifted the lid of the casket.

For what seemed like an eternity, in a split second Orion felt he had been hurled into a blind, unfathomable abyss where life and living were merely an afterthought, where pain was measured by its depth. A scream formed within Orion until he cried aloud, "Oh my God!"

In the sterile coffin lay the body of Orion Eckley Darnel.

The die had been cast. I had created a fictional character who would live and breath and love—then "DIE" and live again. This was **not** the story of Elvis Presley, because, after all, Elvis was gone, wasn't he?

Prior to writing Chapter One I wrote the Epilogue:

EPILOGUE

An ordinary looking late-model station wagon, piled high with gray plastic trunks, turned slowly onto Interstate

40. The driver was a handsome man with a reddish-brown beard; he wore dark sun-glasses. Beside him sat a young woman, her hair tied into pony-tails. She wore no make-up. Neither spoke, but listened to a song on the car radio. It had been written only minutes after the death of Orion Darnell, and was already a smash hit. It was called "Orion."

*"You came from out of nowhere with your haunting melody
We laughed and cried and screamed and tried to touch our fantasy.
You danced and sang your way into the hearts that cry for you.
Cause, now we cry, Orion, what did we do to you?*

*Orion, we chased after you while following a dream
But now the dream is echoed in the songs you loved to sing.
To those who listen close a note of sadness whispers through
Orion, what did we do to you?*

*You opened up your soul to let us see your love light shine
And we were glad to take your gift but gave no peace of mind.
We never got the chance to say goodbye, God be with you,
And now you're gone Orion, what did we do to you?"*

Smiling with joy the man reached over and touched the woman's cheek. They both glanced at the child in the back, asleep on a pillow, a happy dream written on her innocent face.

Another car turned onto Interstate 40. It was long and black and sleek. The man behind the wheel chewed lazily on an unlit cigar. He was heading toward Memphis. Several weeks ago he had seen a young man perform at a small club. The boy was untrained, unpolished, but there was something in his voice, some new sound . . .*

---

*The song "Orion" was written by Carol Halupke after the first draft of the novel was complete and then worked into the Epilogue.

Orion, although dead to the millions who mourned him, now lived. The thought that the anagram of the name Elvis is the word "lives" made me smile. Orion's Epilogue was an eternal shrine to that anagram: birth to death to birth. All I need do was write the in-between, flesh in the skeleton, make ORION **live.**

This was 1977. Few books were out on Elvis, although ELVIS: WHAT HAPPENED, penned by close friends of Elvis', had been released shortly before Elvis' "death." I don't know if that book was yet in the bookstores by August 16, 1977. No matter. I wasn't trying to write about Elvis as a particular person, but rather I was trying to capture the essence of a soul via my imagination. Creatively I wanted to interpret a phenomenon, a legend, a mortal who had become a Musical Messiah. I wondered as I went to bed that night what I would indeed write about to flesh in that skeleton, to give substance to something still somewhat fuzzy and distant in my mind?

I boned up on mythology, read key passages in the Bible, and then picked up my favorite book of poems, THE BEST LOVED POEMS OF THE AMERICAN PEOPLE, which included the works of Tennyson, Kipling, Browning, and Emerson. Randomly I turned to a poem I never recall reading. I found my substance.

"I am standing on the threshold of eternity at last,
As reckless of the future as I have been of the past;
I am void of all ambition, I am dead of every hope;
The coil of life is ended; I am letting go the rope.

I have drifted down the stream of life til weary, sore oppressed;
And I'm tired of all the motion and simply want to rest.
I have tested all the pleasures that life can hold for man.
I have scanned the whole world over til there's nothing left to
*   scan.*

I have heard the finest music, I have read the rarest books,
I have drunk the purest vintage, I have tasted all the cooks;
I have run the scale of living and have sounded every tone,
There is nothing left to live for and I long to be alone.

Alone and unmolested
    where the vultures do not rave
And the only refuge left me
    is the quiet, placid grave. . . . ."
(On the Threshold—Poet Unkown
    from
The Best Loved Poems of The American People)

I also found it strange that the one poem I turned to is one of the few in this book listed as "Poet Unknown."

Because I was **not** trying to write about Elvis specifically, I decided to use the story of Jesus (the King) together with mythology and create a contemporary hero, a man who via music was given "the gift of tongues," (since it is said that music is a universal language).

I stress this fact often because of the many books that appeared on Elvis Presley **after** ORION was copyrighted. At that moment I had no conscious knowledge that Elvis saw himself psychically connected with Jesus. This will be explained in a later chapter which deals with Elvis and the Jesus connection.

Not only was I using Biblical and mythological symbolism, but I would rely on Dr. Hugh Schonfield's THE PASSOVER PLOT which outlined what may be the greatest conspiracy in the history of mankind: the hoaxing of the death of Jesus of Nazareth. I would fictionally equate this theory: the hoaxing of the death of Orion of Nashville.

As was written in the Biblical stories concerning the life of Jesus, I would take ORION from the time he floated peacefully in the waters of his mother's womb through an amazing life journey, a mortal standing on the edge of eternity, a beloved king who had run "the scale of living and had sounded every tone"—a man hunted by the masses, a man who would lead a second and safe life, "unmolested."

Having long been a student of various religions and mythology, I believe in the power of threes: the tri-power, the power of the Trinity. I began with Jess the father, Dixie the sacred mother, Orion the blessed son whom God had promised, equalling Joseph, Mary and Jesus. Biblical settings such as Antioch were used as well as a combination of Biblical and mythological names: Tucker Joshua as Orion's closest friend

15

(Joshua is sometimes another name for John, meaning a "warrior of divine appointment"). Tuck would be the warrior who would protect Orion from the mobs. He would also seemingly be Orion's Judas.*

---

*Because of the psychic significance involved in the writing of ORION, together with all that materialized later, I have written a thesis on the creation of this novel. It details step-by-step how each central character was conceived such as his or her storyline and places. Without a doubt it proves that ORION was not copied after the life of Elvis Presley but rather that Elvis Presley's life contains a universal theme. This statement will be proven as my story unravels. Many who have read ORION, including many close to Elvis and his parents, say I captured the essence of Elvis Presley's soul and that of those close to him. Yet on a more basic plane, I actually captured and wrote about specific events and conversations in Elvis' life—events and conversations later biographically written in books released long **after** ORION was copyrighted and released.

CATE OF COPYRIGHT REGISTRATION

This certificate. issued under the seal of the Copyright Office in accordance with the provisions of section 410(a) of title 17. United States Code. attests that copyright registration has been made for the work identified below. The information in this certificate has been made a part of the Copyright Office records.

Barbara Ringer

Register of Copyrights
United States of America

FORM TX

REGISTRATION NUMBER

TXu   B-038

TX   TXU

EFFECTIVE DATE OF REGISTRATION

JUN 15 1976
Month   Day   Year

DO NOT WRITE ABOVE THIS LINE. IF YOU NEED MORE SPACE, USE CONTINUATION SHEET

①
Title

TITLE OF THIS WORK:

ORION

PREVIOUS OR ALTERNATIVE TITLES:

If a periodical or serial give Vol ...... No ...... Issue Date ......

PUBLICATION AS A CONTRIBUTION: (If this work was published as a contribution to a periodical, serial or collection. give information about the collective work in which the contribution appeared.)

If published in a periodical or serial give: Vol ...... No ...... Date ...... Pages ......

Title of Collective Work: ......

A PLACE TO BE BORN

The first draft of ORION was written within fifty-four days; the book often seemed to "write itself." It was officially copyrighted in June of 1978. This is important in light of the events to occur, events I wrote as fiction—events that began to come true **after** the fact. ORION is definitely a case of life imitating art.

This draft was given to Carole Halupke, a friend and songwriter, who suggested sending a copy of the manuscript to Mae Boren Axton, whom Carole knew. Not being part of the music world, I did not know that Mae played a pivotal role in the life of Elvis. She worked with the Colonel, introduced Elvis to his famous manager, played P.R. lady and is generally regarded as the Grand Dame of Nashville.

Mae Axton also co-wrote Elvis' first million dollar hit, HEARTBREAK HOTEL.

Naturally I was a bit nervous about having this first draft seen by anyone, let alone someone of the stature of Mae. I agreed and within a short time Mae telephoned. "I can't believe what you've written," Mae expressed. "How do you know so much?"

We discussed the fact I had never been to Memphis or Nashville. "Then how did you write about it so accurately?" she questioned.

"I don't know. It just happened . . . ?" I further explained that ORION was fiction and that I knew very little about Elvis Presley. Most of the biographies written about Elvis were written after my copyright on ORION, thus I had no research source, had I intentionally wished to imitate Elvis' life. This truth is essential to remember. I discussed with Mae the tri-power theory, the Jesus/Mythology/Elvis connection and a basic insight into how the novel was born.

"You may not have known Elvis personally," Mae stated. "but you have uncannily captured not only the essence of his soul, but the soul of his mother, his father—even the Colonel . . ."

Mae again wondered how I knew so much. "I saw some of the events you write about, things no one knew. You even described Orion's favorite sandwich as peanut butter, banana and mayonnaise."

I had not yet met Mae in person but an intimacy and warmth was quickly developing. Both of us mentioned more than once how familiar we seemed. We continued discussing the novel ORION. With all that eventually happened, one of the bright spots was Mae. (I have agreed to write her book, INSIDE HEARTBREAK HOTEL. I like the idea because it's an inside look into the world of country music.)

"ORION is the only book I'll give a testimony to," she offered—which she did and which was used on the promotions sent out by both the hardback and paperback publishers. I was understandably curious as to why Mae, who was very close to Elvis, would give a testimony to a fictional book whose hero hoaxes his death. When I questioned her, she replied after a pause, "I believe Elvis is dead . . . but anything is possible . . ."

Since Mae and I had discussed the fact I had captured certain incidents and characteristic traits with accuracy, the thought did cross my mind about Elvis' death not being as it appeared. Little did I know what would eventually be revealed. We also talked about Mae's last conversation with Elvis pre-August 16, 1977. "He telephoned me about nine days before the sixteenth in tears. He had just read the galleys from the book ELVIS: WHAT HAPPENED? written by his close friends, Red and Sonny West and Dave Hebler. He said three words that broke my heart: 'Mae, it hurts . . .' "

Mae was one of the few people who possessed the unlisted number for Elvis's private "red telephone." She also gave Elvis one-third interest in HEARTBREAK HOTEL, which she wrote with Tommy Durden. "Elvis never claimed to write a word or note of that song, and he never asked for any

19

from the desk of
Mae Boren Axton

Feb. 10, 1978

Thanks for sending me the script of the
book "Orion". I realize it's fiction, but
I saw my dear friend Elvis on each page
I read. I have been the recipient of
several scripts and stories based on Elvis
and this is the one I consider the most
apropos. In fact it would be a terrific
movie.

Congratulations!!

Sincerely,

Mae Boren Axton

MAE BOREN AXTON
Public Relations Consultant

49 Music Square West, Suite 303
Nashville, Tennessee 37203
(615) 327-0221

February 13, 1978

Dear Gail:

Yes, indeed, I'd love a story on me, thank you so much for offering to do one. I'm sending you some material that has been done on me. I'm also sending a copy of the <u>first</u> of three books on singers.

Your other letter accompanying the rest of the script was so beautiful I had tears in my eyes...for you to say "yours means the most". His mother was a very wonderful lady, and this love was so special. I'm so glad that someone is finally doing a story, though fiction, so much "The Elvis Presley Story, done so tenderly. I've read so many, but this is the first one that I really felt put the finger on the pulse. I like the melding of the humor, the sad, and the tragic. He was indeed "The King", though he didn't like to be called that. I also loved the "hope" and the "winning".

As a writer myself, I agree that writers are very sensitive, and I know you put your heart and soul into this creation. In reading it, I cried <u>with</u> you.

God bless you, I have come to feel I know you well, and I will show this script in movie circles.

Sincerely,

Mae Boren Axton

MBA:ah

rights. I just told Tommy that we should give him a third because Elvis was poor. Tommy said it was fine with him."

Mae was always hesitant in conversation with me about the possibility that my work of fiction might indeed be fact. Some intuition on my part made me back off from pressing her. Still, she shared information. "Elvis had been suffering from glaucoma," she offered. "Not many know about this. It's strange that you wrote Orion was having problems with his eyes . . ."

By early spring Carole and her husband Walt, and my husband Carm and I, went to Nashville to meet Mae. The secret of our "familiarity" became clear: Mae Boren Axton taught at the same school I attended as a teenager! I recognized her immediately. Normally we know our teachers by Mrs. so-and-so—thus her full name had not clicked. She had known me by another name. I could not believe it. While I was a ponytailed teenager with writing aspirations, Mae was in the midst of directing the destiny of a young greased-back, ducktailed singer, for whom she would co-write a song that would rock the world: HEARTBREAK HOTEL. That Mae and I had come full circle is an understatement—yet it was only step one in the most incredible Elvis Presley story ever told.

Prior to our meeting in Nashville, Mae suggested I send a copy of the manuscript to Bob Neal, a personal friend of hers and also head of the William Morris Agency in Nashville. The William Morris Agency is thought by many to be the most prestigious and powerful talent and literary agency in the world. For Mae to intercede on my behalf appeared to be a marvelous career move. I learned that Bob Neal had also played a pivotal role in Elvis' destiny. Originally he had been a D.J. in Memphis and later was known as "Elvis' first manager" before he sold Elvis' contract to Colonel Tom Parker. Mae suggested that Bob's reaction would be valuable and secondly, William Morris' representation would be an asset in securing book and movie rights. As you'll note by Mae's letter, she thought ORION would make a wonderful movie and she offered to show it to movie people.

My excitement grew. Although I had written professionally for years, ORION was the first novel I had completed. I knew that the William Morris Agency would be picky about taking on new talent and it worried me that they would be seeing a raw manuscript. I took a chance and sent a copy to

NEW YORK
BEVERLY HILLS
CHICAGO
NASHVILLE
LONDON
ROME
MUNICH

WILLIAM MORRIS AGENCY, INC. | ESTABLISHED 1898 | XXXX
2325 CRESTMOOR ROAD · NASHVILLE, TENNESSEE 37215 · (615) 385-0310

February 24, 1978

Dear Gail:

Received your letter of February 18 along with the script that you sent to me.

In order to have the script reviewed here or by our New York or Beverly Hills office, we have to have a signed release on the matter. I'm enclosing two copies of this release for you. Please sign the release and return to me so we can proceed with having the script reviewed.

Best personal regards,

WILLIAM MORRIS AGENCY, INC.

Bob Neal

jh

encl.

NEW YORK
BEVERLY HILLS
CHICAGO
NASHVILLE
LONDON
ROME
MUNICH

WILLIAM MORRIS AGENCY, INC.
2325 CRESTMOOR ROAD · NASHVILLE, TENNESSEE 37215 · (615) 385-0310

ESTABLISHED 1898

XXXX

March 14, 1978

Dear Gail:

After receiving your release I've finally been able to complete reading ORION. To be perfectly honest with you, I was quite fascinated
by the treatment, particularly the ending.

I have spoken to our office in New York and the manuscript is on the
way to them. I emphasized that they should give it quick attention.

I'll be back in touch with you as quickly as I get an evaluation from
New York.

Best regards,

WILLIAM MORRIS AGENCY, INC.

Bob Neal

jh

Bob Neal. When Bob telephoned me his initial reaction was similar to Mae's. He also asked how I knew so much?

Bob and I spoke often and we corresponded. He asked if he could send the manuscript to the New York office? I was a bit nervous about the condition of a manuscript and agreed as long as the people in New York were told it was a first draft.

As you will note by Bob's letter, he paid specific attention to the "ending" of ORION, which is the hoaxing of a death. When we talked over the telephone he also mentioned how fascinating he found the ending.

Finally, Mel Berger from William Morris' New York office telephoned expressing similar enthusiasm for ORION. At one point I mentioned to Mel that some associates wished to show ORION to move contacts. Mel left me with the impression that I shouldn't pass the manuscript around or let too many people see it outside William Morris. Bob Neal stressed that it would not be a good idea to let too many people see it.

Prior to William Morris' advice of not showing ORION to anyone, I had already allowed others to see it. Some were associates of Carole Halupke's. At that time we were discussing having a demo done on the song ORION. These people do not fit into the overall plot other than, as the letters show, I agreed to William Morris' request to get all copies back as it was obvious they did not want "other eyes" to view this project. I was very appreciative of their attention and did not want to annoy them. In truth I was intimidated. Still, this was only 1978. I was trusting, naive and certainly enjoyed believing that I had written something special.

The portion of my letter to Bob mentioning the name "Dave Gersheson" came as a result of having met with Ed Spivia, then head of the Georgia Film Commission and now with his own production company. Since Burt Reynolds had done a great deal of filming in Georgia, Ed had worked with him. Dave Gersheson is an associate of Burt Reynolds and makes many film decisions. Ed had a positive reaction to ORION and also thought it would make an interesting film. The project wasn't meant as one for Burt Reynolds to star in but to direct. At this point I was using as many contacts as possible, including Mervyn LeRoy.

At about this time, Atlanta attorney Joel Katz, an entertainment lawyer from Macon, contacted me. He had also been

As I said I can't recall when the telephone call came from the west coast Morris office. All my calendar reflects is a notation in the back: "a Mr. Lassfoggle called/Wm. Mrs. W.C."

I now know his name was Abe Lastfogel, but I only found that out years later. As I recall he was pleasant. He knew about ORION as he and Bob Neal had been talking about it. In a nice way he suggested I not show the project around if William Morris were to get involved. I understood his concern, explained that much of what was happening occurred simultaneously and that it was not my intention to put them in a strange position if I signed with them.

There were other telephone calls and letters, some from Bob, some from Mel. They came to me, to Bill, to Joel. Bob Neal repeated it was standard practice to sign an exclusive for three years. What was my decision? Why hadn't I signed the representation papers? I continued to hesitate, although I could in no way define my hesitation.

By now I had three attorneys involved: Bill Carlisle and Neal Boortz (Bill's partner whom I met when Neal was a top talk show host with WRNG radio) and Joel Katz. A conference call came in from William Morris to Joel. Besides myself, Carole and Walt Halupke were among those present. "When was I going to sign the representation papers?" was the nature of the call.

I didn't want to make a wrong move, yet I felt very uncomfortable. Even in late August I was hesitating. Finally I drew back and turned in another direction, without being convinced that I wasn't making a mistake. Would I ruin my career before it was launched? Would I be penalized? Why was I so uneasy? Yet history had taught me that I must follow instincts and trust myself, trust also that if I had indeed via fiction tapped into something explosive, then it might follow that this feeling had a basis.

Mel was not happy about my decision. He said he had already put effort and energy into selling ORION, had even shown it to some publishers; thus, I need not fear it sitting gathering dust. I found this surprising since I made it clear ORION was still in its first draft. And also, why would William Morris show it when I had not signed the all-important three year exclusive?

As you'll note letters continued to come:

30

given a copy of ORION and said he would like to be involved. Despite the fact I had a personal attorney, I welcomed both his attention and advice. Thus, the-people-who-wanted-involvement picture enlarges. Today I certainly would not advise going out in as many directions as I had. Back then I was excited and easily impressed—young and more often than not, just plain stupid.

Perhaps it was the mention of other movie people that prompted a telephone call from the west coast Morris office. I can't recall if this call came before or after I went to New York accompanied by my attorney, Bill Carlisle. We did go to New York though and met with Mel Berger and a William Morris attorney. Bill and I were impressed by Mel Berger. He was young, efficient and crisp—very New Yorkish. But as before, I felt somewhat intimidated by the plush Morris offices on the Avenue of the Americas—expensive furniture, quiet, resembling a lawyer's office, somewhat overpowering in its understatement. (Since Mel was young I don't know how he fit in or who gave him the ORION project, but I do know from my conversations with Bob Neal that Bob had originally contacted someone else at William Morris/New York.)

Before coming to New York, Mel had asked that I sign representation papers. In our New York meeting Mel again asked that I sign a three year exclusive with them. Both Bill and I asked, "If a three year exclusive is signed, who is to say ORION won't lie gathering dust for three years?" I knew enough back then that if I signed, my hands would be tied and I would be prohibited from showing ORION to anyone. Mel promised this would not occur, that signing a three-year exclusive was standard for William Morris, that this was the only way they did business. (I've been told that this is not the *only* way they do business.)

Rather than sign the representation papers, Bill and I decided to further review the situation back in Atlanta. Later that day Bill, my husband Carm (who had gone to New York with us) and I discussed events. We had put William Morris off and hoped that wasn't a mistake. They were giants in the literary world. We also shared a feeling of "something happening beneath the surface." I was not famous or powerful enough to warrant this type of courtship. I felt uneasy, "a David standing in the shadow of Goliath."

NEW YORK
BEVERLY HILLS
CHICAGO
NASHVILLE
LONDON
ROME
MUNICH

WILLIAM MORRIS AGENCY, INC.
2325 CRESTMOOR ROAD · NASHVILLE, TENNESSEE 37215 · (615) 385-0310

March 28, 1978

Dear Gail:

Thanks for your letter of March 27th.

Fred Foster is out of town--I think he's in Europe. I'll check with him when he gets back in. In the meanwhile, I stopped by Bob Ray's office and picked up his copy of ORION and am forwarding it to Mel Berger this afternoon.

Best regards,

WILLIAM MORRIS AGENCY, INC.

Bob Neal

jh

March 27, 1976

Mr. Bob Neal
President
William Morris Agency
2325 Crestmoor Road
Nashville, Tenn. 30215

Dear Bob:

Thanks so very much for your nice telephone call the other day. Mel
Berger did indeed get in touch with me. He said "Orion" is a "phenomenon.

Mel also asked me for more photocopies of "Orion" so I placed a telephone
call to both Fred Foster (Monument Records - 241-6565) and Bob Bray
(Celebrity Management 244-0116) but neither were in. They each have
a copy and I thought that perhaps they could send them on to either you or
Mel but no luck? Do you know either of them? Would it help if you called
them? I think that Mel wants to "gather in his fold" any loose manuscripts
floating around and I don't bleame him. I'll send Mel a copy of this letter
so that he can also follow up. Dave Gersheson (Burt Reynold's agent in
California has one too 213-278-2343) also has a copy. At this point I believe the majority of these should be in the hands of William Morris.

Bob, I cannot tell you how appreciative I am of your interest in the script.
I realize that none of this would have worked had not the manuscript had
something to offer but even the best of works are often hidden due to the
right people not viewing them. If there is any way I can repay this favor
please do not hesitate to call me. As soon as everything is locked up as
far as a book and movie contract go I plan to make a special trip to Nashville in order to meet both you and Mae. The least I can do is to take you
to dinner althought that will by no means settle my debt!

Have a wonderful day and thanks as always,

Gail Brewer-Giorgio

NEW YORK
BEVERLY HILLS
CHICAGO
NASHVILLE
LONDON
ROME
MUNICH

WILLIAM MORRIS AGENCY, INC. ESTABLISHED 1898
1350 AVENUE OF THE AMERICAS · NEW YORK, N.Y. 10019 · (212) 586-5100 XXXX

Cable Address
"WILLMORRIS"
TELEX 670165

June 23, 1978

Mr. Robert O. Loftis, Jr.
Katz, Weissman & Loftis, P.C.
Suite B-130
5775 Peachtree Dunwoody Road, N.E.
Atlanta, Georgia 30342

Dear Mr. Loftis:

I was quite surprised and confused to receive your
note of June 20 as I had been under the impression
that I was representing Gail Brewer-Giorgio in connection with the publication of her novel, ORION.
At least, that was what I had been told by Gail and
by Joel Katz who has been in the process of working
with Jim Arnoff on Gail's William Morris authoriza-
tion papers. If there has been a change, I have not
been notified and I would appreciate immediate clar-
ification on this point as I am still actively talking
about this novel to reprinters.

As for the quotation, given my position at William
Morris I cannot authorize the use of my name or the
Agency. It is a good quote though as it is an excellent novel. If you can find someone else to echo
these words, they are yours.

Sincerely,

WILLIAM MORRIS AGENCY, INC.

Mel Berger
/dp
cc: Joel Katz
    Gail Brewer-Giorgio
    Jim Arnoff
    Bob Neal

NEW YORK
BEVERLY HILLS
CHICAGO
NASHVILLE
LONDON
ROME
MUNICH

WILLIAM MORRIS AGENCY, INC.
1350 AVENUE OF THE AMERICAS · NEW YORK, N.Y. 10019 · (212) 586-5100   XXXX

Cable Address
"WILLMORRIS"
TELEX 620168

August 4, 1978

Dear Gail:

I would very much like to resolve our representation
status of you and your works.

Would you please have your attorneys send us all the
papers we discussed last week.

Sincerely,

Mel Berger
/dp

As I proceeded, I was filled with doubts as to whether I had made a horrendous mistake. Right or wrong, the decision had been made, and I directed my efforts elsewhere. The ORION project seemed too complicated. Too many people were involved—too many people telling me what I should or should not do. How I wished I could go back to square one, start all over.

By 1979 I had signed with a hardback publisher. Almost simultaneously emerged a singer named "Orion." Strangely, he was on the SUN RECORDS label, which was Elvis Presley's early label. Characters from my novel ORION were used in full, including the Prologue. This appeared on the back of the first Orion album REBORN. Details such as "Dixie-Land" and "Mac Weiman" were used—Dixie-Land as the place to write Orion; Mac Weiman as the man who guided Orion. (In my novel ORION, Dixie-Land is Orion's home; Mac Weiman is Orion's manager/agent.) I also noted that my fictious character was the co-writer of at least two songs, LONESOME ANGEL and WASHING MACHINE.

Orion Eckley Darnell was the full name of a character I created in 1977 and had copyrighted in 1978.

Orion sounded so much like Elvis Presley that it was amazing. The voice on some *songs* sounded identical to Elvis. Orion wore a mask and upon the release of the first album was causing a major controversy. But Orion was *not* Elvis. I knew this from the moment I was introduced to him. His name is Jimmy Ellis. In fact both Orion and SUN RECORDS made a deliberate effort to send out promotional material emphatically denying that Elvis Presley or anyone connected with Elvis had anything to do with the singer Orion. The fact is no claim was made that Orion was Elvis "reborn." I was told that the album title was chosen because the songs on that particular album dealt with rebirth. A second and very important fact is that Jimmy Ellis, whether a masked Orion or not, has an incredible voice and performing talent. Although one may think he is pantomiming Elvis' voice, he is actually using his own voice, one that happens to sound like Elvis. The fact he chose to perform under the name of a character from a book of fiction does not make him less real. He could have chosen to come out under the name of "John Smith" and the controversy would have been the same. It was his voice that was on trial. To this day I feel that too many people were looking for a flaw in the talent while forgetting the quality of the talent. Looking for a flaw, many D.J.'s began questioning who was really behind the mask. Fans even asked if it was Elvis?

"No," said Orion and SUN RECORDS.

"Is it someone trying to make everyone think it's Elvis?"

"No," came the reply. "The singer Orion is a very private person. Beyond providing the singer with privacy, the mask is Orion's trademark just as wigs are Dolly Parton's."

Having met Jimmy Ellis/Orion, I can testify to the truth he is private, rather shy and never seemed in need of income. In fact it appeared the exact opposite. Although he was constantly sought after to perform, to give interviews, to appear on radio and television, he, for the main pulled back. For this he was sometimes disliked, called arrogant and in some instances called a "fake." This type of reasoning is beyond my realm of thinking. Is Michelangelo a fake on the basis he is not a Leonardo? Isn't there room for both, despite the fact they are constantly compared?

I, too, was continually asked who Orion was. Respecting his privacy I said, "He's Orion."

"But how can you be sure he's not Elvis?"

"Because I saw him without his mask, and I know his true identity. He is *not* Elvis."

Another question was, "How can you be sure that the man-with-the-mask pictured on the Orion album covers is the same voice singing on the albums? You can't see a voice."

That was the kind of "damned if I do and damned if do not type of question." I had *never* been in the studio when Orion cut his albums. There were times I wondered the same thing. Also, I entertained the thought that there might be two voices on the albums. I knew that whatever answer I gave I would set myself up for possible accusations, such as this was nothing more than a promotional scheme to sell my novel. I faced such a question this past August of 1987 on Y-106 Radio in Atlanta. It was toward the end of the program when I had been on for three or four hours and the interviewer had been asking me questions about the novel ORION, the book-about-the-book, the mystery tape and miscellaneous information. Prior to being on the air, I had, by invitation, met with the interviewer and his producer. They told me what they wanted to talk about and asked that I not digress or go off on tangents. Never once did they mention wanting to discuss the singer Orion in connection with my novel. Had they, I would have made clear to them that SUN RECORDS and I never had a contract. I would have also showed them copies of letters written by my attorney Bill Carlisle about this. As it was, I felt "sneaked upon"—as though I were "guilty by association." Since the singer Orion had received much media and radio attention, surely they must have known I was not trying to hide the existence of this masked singer. Yet I felt as though someone were deliberately trying to trap me. It's a strange position to be in. If I discuss the singer, who has since disappeared, it might look as though I'm involved in a scam, or as the interviewer delicately put it, "a marketing ploy done in the name of entertainment."

If I don't bring up the singer Orion, then it is assumed I'm covering up something. Either way I can be made to look devious. It's almost like having your car stolen and then being blamed if it's involved in a mishap. it's your car, but you were not the driver.

To be fair to these Y-106 gentlemen, they were not in possession of this book since it was being written at the time. The interviewer was trying to remain neutral, although I don't think he was. Toward the end of the interview, he began to use terminology such as "your association with the singer" and the phrase "set-up" which made negative assumptions. I suppose had I gone on the air "cold," without having previously met with them and taken their advice as to what *they* wished to emphasize, it wouldn't be a sensitive point with me. They knew that I was not on the show to sell the novel ORION. I had no book to sell, because it had mysteriously disappeared. I agreed to give them hours of my time because I was asked to appear. I never asked them. Also, since they surprised me with the Orion albums during the last few minutes of the show, their assumptions may have left an erroneous impression on the listeners. I felt somewhat like a rape victim being reprimanded for having lost her virginity!

The questions continued about Orion-the-masked-singer.

"Was Orion a front for Elvis?"

"Was it Elvis' voice on the albums and Orion's face on the album covers?"

"Why was Orion on the same record label as Elvis once was?"

"Why is Orion's record producer a man named Bobby Smith? Doesn't Elvis have a cousin by that name?"

"Why are Orion's costumes designed by the same designer as Elvis?"

Still unaware of what I would soon discover, I replied by saying the entire SUN episode was a promotional attempt to make the public believe a fictitious story had come to life. I shied away from mentioning that SUN RECORDS had never signed an agreement with me to use any of the novel's material on their albums. It's not that I totally objected but since the project belonged to me, I wanted control. Therefore, a trip to Nashville with my attorney again was imperative. Carole and Walt Halupke went with us. We met with SUN RECORDS and discussed the record company's use of my material, such as names and places that were copyrighted under the novel ORION. We needed some sort of contract, some guidelines spelled out. The conversation ended with, "So sue us."

I could only stop them by a lawsuit. It was clearly pointed out by SUN that all this publicity would help sell the novel, that a mystique was being created. It was not hard to tell that a great deal of money was behind the singer: expensive costumes, jewelry, white Cadillac, large bus, a band—the works. Plus Orion was a sensational entertainer and was in his short public existence causing more than a few ripples. I saw him perform at a country fair in Marietta, and the crowds had to be held back by the police. Still, it bothered everyone connected with me that we had no agreement with SUN, and thus no control over how the singer was presented or promoted. But we did not want to sue either. To enter any type of litigation, whether I was a victim or not, could forever put the project on "hold."

More than once the thought crossed my mind that the SUN/Orion connection could eventually lessen my credibility, integrity, and turn the novel into a spoof. On the other hand, it was intriguing and interesting. One magazine named Orion as the entertainer of the year. PM Magazine filmed his show. Bob Greene of the Chicago Tribune wrote about Orion, as did syndicated columnists James Bacon. Orion was getting excellent reviews as an entertainer . . . yet the Elvis question always came up.

The promotional tie-in was intriguing, but I was very uneasy. I felt too small to fight SUN RECORDS—the feeling of "David in the shadow of Goliath" came over me again.

What I couldn't fathom was *why* all of this over a book of fiction? What would Margaret Mitchell have done if one day she answered a knock at her door and there stood Rhett Butler? Surely no work of fiction had ever gone through such unorthodox twists?

I suppose, too, that by not legally stopping SUN RECORDS, such non-action could be construed as consent.

Neither my attorney nor I knew what to do. This was 1979 and ORION had not yet hit the big market. The singer, though, was appearing. When the novel was released, SUN RECORDS began promoting it and then worked a deal out with the hardback publisher to offer the novel for sale through fan clubs, concert tours, and special appearances. SUN RECORDS purchased the hardbacks at the same wholesale price as the bookstores. I never earned any money whatsoever from the SUN connection.

The more ORION appeared, the more mobbed he was. Soon bodyguards were hired. Then suddenly Orion would disappear for long periods of time.

My telephone constantly rang with calls from curious people asking the following questions:

"Who is Orion?"

"Why was Orion seen at Graceland?"

"Who is the power and the money behind Orion?"

"Why are there *two* Orions?"

That question drew me to a halt. "What?" I replied. "I don't understand what you're talking about?"

"I saw two masked men. I was allowed up the steps of Orion's bus, maybe too soon. I almost got to the step when a bodyguard pushed me back, but not before I glanced to my left. I caught a glimpse of **two** Orions, two masked men, both about the same height and weight and both wearing identical costumes. The one who was standing looked at me and then quickly ducked into what I guess was the bus' bathroom. The other one, who was sitting on the edge of the bus' seat rose, walked toward me and came down the steps, sort of backing me off. Then he said hello and began signing autographs," reported a fan.

This didn't make sense. Why **two** Orions? "What did you say to the one who signed autographs?"

"I froze. I mean, I don't know what's going on. I was nervous, scared. I thought since you wrote the book you'd know about this?"

"I can promise you, I know nothing," I stated truthfully.

I mentioned this to Carole Halupke, who replied. "I'm certain there are two Orions. Until you told me this I didn't know what to make of it, but Jimmy Ellis (Orion) told me there were two. It seems he was singing at one place, and in another place—several states away, another masked Orion was also appearing. Jimmy acted like he did not know who the other Orion was. He sort of laughed it off. I thought it was just rumor."

"I can't believe this," I exclaimed in shock. "Do you mean that the Orion we know as Jimmy Ellis was singing in one town and at the same time in another town sang another Orion?"

"I think it's true, Gail. Jimmy said it was true. And when I showed doubt he said for me to check with SUN RECORDS, that it was true."

"Then SUN knows?"

"They know. But I don't know if they're involved."

I shook my head. I couldn't believe it! All of this from fifty-four days of fiction!

I then began to backtrack. Prior to my novel ORION grabbing the attention of SUN RECORDS, SUN had released an album entitled: DUETS, Jerry Lee Lewis and Friends, release date 1978. The country music world was startled by this release because the "friend" on the album was unmistakably Elvis. Jerry Lee and Elvis started at SUN and were friends. I heard rumors that RCA was very upset with SUN over this album since RCA owned the Elvis masters. Then along comes the novel ORION with SUN releasing Orion albums, yet **sending** out promotional material which stated that Orion was actually the "friend" on the DUETS album with Jerry Lee. This is well and fine except for a story by syndicated columnist James Bacon featuring this headline:

ELVIS DEBATE CONTINUES

"The mail won't stop on that column about Elvis Presley of a few weeks back. You know, the one that said Elvis was the mystery singer on the Jerry Lee Lewis record 'Save The Last Dance For Me.' (From the DUETS album.)

So far I have the word of Elvis himself and Red West, a member of Elvis' Memphis Mafia, and both said Elvis just went into the Sun Recording Studios in Memphis and did it to help out an old friend. Elvis said he was unbilled on the record for a very good reason—he was under contract to RCA at the time.

This probably happened sometime in the 1960's and Jerry Lee is not talking because of the contract situation.

One letter from Fresno says the record is a Jerry Lee Lewis hoax—that the singer is trying to get the public to believe it's Elvis. That's hard to believe because Jerry Lee Lewis is one of the big names in country music and he doesn't need hoaxes to get attention.

Another called it a hoax to promote an Elvis imitator—Jimmy Ellis. This letter says Ellis overdubbed the original Jerry Lee Lewis recording and will make a big announcement soon.

Most of the letters come from Elvis fans who all say it is the King himself on the record. One writer comments:

'There are dozens who can sing like Elvis, but no one pronounces words like him. I have played the record a hundred times and I know it is Elvis.'

Of course, there is that group that refuses to believe Elvis is dead—that his death was a hoax. These people all believe it is Elvis on the record, but that it was recorded since Elvis died.

What I don't understand is how anyone could insist that the record is a hoax, or that it proves Elvis is still alive. After all, Elvis himself admitted to me that he did the recording with Jerry Lee Lewis. That eliminates any chance of an imitator. And, since Elvis was still very much alive at the time he told me about the record, it's obvious the record was cut before his death was reported and thus does not prove a thing."

There is absolutely no reason to believe that what he says about Elvis admitting to him that he cut the record with Jerry Lee is anything but true.

Keeping this in mind, why in 1979 did SUN RECORDS release promotional material stating that DUETS, Jerry Lee Lewis and Friends (featuring "Save The Last Dance for Me") was a new "Orion" release?

Why was Orion claiming the album when it is Elvis' voice? Why was the album listed as a new release when actually it was released a year earlier in 1978? Why had SUN RECORDS kept the identity of the "friend" a secret in 1978 but then announced *who* it was in 1979? I knew one of the answers: SUN RECORDS did not know of the novel ORION when they released the DUETS album. Although my novel had been copyrighted in 1978, it had not been released. Still, the name of Jimmy Ellis was mentioned in the James Bacon article. Why, if Jimmy Ellis was with SUN, didn't SUN simply say in 1978 that the "friend" was Ellis? After all, they said in 1979 that Orion was Jimmy Ellis. Or, was there more to this than met the eye? Since I had already heard there were **two** Orions, perhaps Jimmy Ellis was a front for someone else, someone who admittedly was Elvis Presley on an album Orion, via SUN RECORDS, later claimed?

Confused? Imagine being in my shoes!

Obviously, this entire enigma became an overtalked issue within my legal group. "I believe there are two Orions," Bill Carlisle admitted in a meeting. "I think there always was. Personally I don't think Elvis died. I think that he planned the whole thing, and that in order to sing now and then he uses a cover. This Jimmy Ellis is his front."

"But I don't think Jimmy is an imitator. He's too talented," I defended. "If he wanted to earn money as an

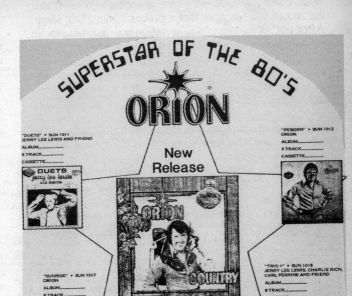

SUN INTERNATIONAL CORPORATION
3106 Belmont Boulevard - Nashville, Tennessee 37212
(615) 385-1960   Telex: 3711222

FALL, 1979

 is definitely not Elvis as the enclosed
article suggests.

 is a tremendous talent that is building a
cult type following emerging from the deep
South and spreading all over the world.

Radio stations that play his records say their requests
are almost unbelievable for a new artist. Small record
stores report sales of 100 or more albums on ORION's
first release REBORN.

The second single release WASHING MACHINE is a giant
where exposed. The name ORION pronounced "O-Ryan" will
be a household word in the 1980's. Concerts and clubs
alike report SRO. His tour started as a 30 day showcase
and is now expanded to 60 days.

We hope you enjoy ORION as much as we did making this
album.

Sincerely,

SUN INTERNATIONAL CORPORATION

SHELBY S. SINGLETON, JR.
President

SSS/rr

cc: Sally Smash
     Micki Foster
     Mac Weiman
     John Singleton

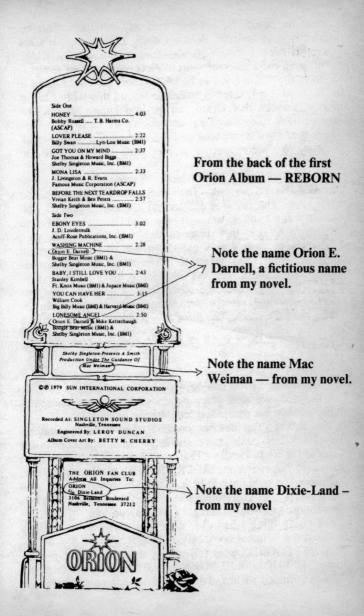

Side One

HONEY 4:03
Bobby Russell ..... T. B. Harms Co.
(ASCAP)

LOVER PLEASE 2:22
Billy Swan ....Lyn-Lou Music (BMI)

GOT YOU ON MY MIND 2:37
Joe Thomas & Howard Biggs
Shelby Singleton Music, Inc. (BMI)

MONA LISA 2:33
J. Livingston & R. Evans
Famous Music Corporation (ASCAP)

BEFORE THE NEXT TEARDROP FALLS
Vivian Keith & Ben Peters 2:57
Shelby Singleton Music, Inc. (BMI)

Side Two

EBONY EYES 3:02
J. D. Loudermilk
Acuff-Rose Publications, Inc. (BMI)

WASHING MACHINE 2:28
Orion E. Darnell
Boggie Bear Music (BMI) &
Shelby Singleton Music, Inc. (BMI)

BABY, I STILL LOVE YOU 2:43
Stanley Kimbell
Ft. Knox Music (BMI) & Jupace Music (BMI)

YOU CAN HAVE HER 3:15
William Cook
Big Billy Music (BMI) & Harvard Music (BMI)

LONESOME ANGEL 2:50
Orion E. Darnell & Mike Ketterbaugh
Boogie Bear Music (BMI) &
Shelby Singleton Music, Inc. (BMI)

*Shelby Singleton-Presents A Smith
Production Under The Guidance Of
Mac Weiman*

©℗ 1979 SUN INTERNATIONAL CORPORATION

Recorded At: SINGLETON SOUND STUDIOS
Nashville, Tennessee
Engineered By: LEROY DUNCAN
Album Cover Art By: BETTY M. CHERRY

THE ORION FAN CLUB
Address All Inquiries To:
ORION
C/o Dixie-Land
3106 Belmont Boulevard
Nashville, Tennessee 37212

ORION

From the back of the first Orion Album — REBORN

Note the name Orion E. Darnell, a fictitious name from my novel.

Note the name Mac Weiman — from my novel.

Note the name Dixie-Land — from my novel

imitator he could. He's better than any out there. But he doesn't have to imitate. He's not doing Elvis songs. It's his voice, his talent . . ."

Bill gave me a paternal smile. "Hear me out. You're right. Orion is too damn good to be an imitator. He could make it on his own. Still, there is someone behind this with a lot of money, enough that Orion can go into hiding anytime he pleases. Hell, they may be related for all we know."

For the fun of it, we took an Elvis picture and drew a mask on him. We were amazed at how little Elvis looked like himself.

"See what I mean," Bill added. "Suppose Elvis wanted to record and even perform. Then suppose there was someone Elvis knew who sounded and looked like him, someone who wasn't really known, someone that might even be related to him. Now he uses this singer to sing on some albums, then Elvis throws in a few songs, then the two of them sing together. Now Elvis wants to perform, so he has Jimmy/Orion wear a mask, gets his designer to make two of everything. One sings, then the other sings. One here, the other there. Sometimes at the same time with one popping on stage, then the other. The mask is a perfect cover. Orion is a perfect cover. If anyone suspects it's Elvis and calls in the authorities, guess who's unmasked? Guess who's fingerprinted?"

"Orion?" I asked meekly.

"His double. Elvis can do what he wants but he's safe."

I laughed. We were playing games but there was an underlying seriousness that asked: could it be possible?

No. It was a fun idea but too far-fetched to believe that my novel ORION could have suddenly become a convenient vehicle for Elvis Presley. That was bizarre. I would have to disregard James Bacon, SUN RECORDS, rumors, questions, sightings. I would have to believe that Orion was exactly who he was and that everything else was either wishful thinking, promotional genius, hoaxing, or even a con job.

The only thing I had ever done was to sit down one day and write a fictional book called ORION.

SUN RECORDS went full-stream ahead with the Orion albums. In 1979 both REBORN and SUNRISE were released. SUN continued to use characters from my novel as though they were real people. I wish I could present the albums with this book. I am in possession of them as are many others. They do exist.

By the time I received a "Bulletin" from SUN RECORDS that was supposed to be a resume of Orion ("Fact or Fiction"), I could only laugh. Somebody was having a marvelous time—*somebody* was either a marketing genius or a prankster. It really was getting comical. But it was also sad. The novel ORION could also be taken as a joke. Anyone who has read it knows it is a sensitive and serious work of fiction. I sighed. This could not continue. I called my attorney. "Bill, I'm afraid ORION is being presented as a parody. It's not my doing, not my desire . . ."

I read him the promotional Bulletin. Everything about the singer Orion came straight from my novel. My work of fiction had "come to life"—but not via the movie screen.

"Maybe *somebody* does not want anyone to take your book seriously," Bill suggested.

"But why?"

"I don't know, Gail," Bill replied sadly. "I don't know."

Orion continued singing. I began doing signings of the first editions. I tried to see the situation as positive, but I was once again uneasy. ORION was out of my control and that was not morally right. Another telephone call came. It was from a Elvis fan club president. The woman asked, "Gail, how many Orions are there?"

My breath caught. Was this never going to end? "One," I replied. "Why do you ask?"

"I believe there are two," she stated firmly. "I've literally seen most of Elvis' road tours. Most of the time I sat up front. Naturally I've been captivated by Orion, but I knew he wasn't Elvis. Although when I listen to some of the songs on Orion's albums, I'm not sure. Some of these songs I swear are sung by Elvis. Anyway, I went to see Orion and I thought he was great. At first I guess I went to see Orion to be reminded of Elvis, but then I was caught up in watching Orion."

"Orion is not trying to be Elvis," I explained what I knew to be true. "He's Orion and I think he should be accepted and judged for his own talent, nothing else."

"True. Let me finish. I was watching Orion and then he

45

SUN INTERNATIONAL CORPORATION
3106 BELMONT BOULEVARD • NASHVILLE, TENNESSEE 37212
(615) 385-1960   TELEX: 3711222

FACT OR FICTION

ORION

NAME:	ORION ECKLEY DARNELL
BORN:	RIBBONSVILLE, TENNESSEE 12/31/36
FATHER:	JESS DARNELL
MOTHER:	DIXIE DARNELL (DECEASED)
WIFE:	DANIELLE
DAUGHTER:	MELE LEILANI - BIRTHDAY 1970
HOME:	DIXIELAND, NASHVILLE, TENNESSEE
MANAGER:	MAC WEIMAN, C/O: DIXIELAND-NASHV1
LABEL:	SUN
LATEST ALBUM:	"ORION" REBORN
HEIGHT:	6'3"
WEIGHT:	185
HAIR:	BLACK
EYES:	BLUE-BLACK
COMPLEXION:	FAIR
FAVORITE COLOR:	WHITE
FAVORITE FOOD:	DOWN HOME SOUTHERN COOKIN'
FAVORITE CAR:	CADILLAC
FAVORITE CLOTHES:	ANYTHING DIFFERENT
HOBBIES:	HAVING FUN
FAVORITE SPORT:	KARATE
EDUCATION:	HIGH SCHOOL-CURTISWOOD-NASHVILLE
BEST FRIEND:	TUCK GAMEREE
AMBITION:	MORE GOLD RECORDS
FAVORITE SONG:	THIS MONTH, "HONEY"

$$$$$$$$$$$
800-251-2052

BULLETIN

went behind the curtain for a quick drink of water. He came back and went into another number. I was sitting close to the stage, and I saw sweat marks under Orion's arms. He stopped singing and said something like, 'excuse me folks, but I need a glass of water.' When he returned, I suddenly felt a jolt. It wasn't the same man! There was no sweat marks and he was only out of sight a few seconds. Then he starts singing. Now Elvis had a way of his backside dimpling when turning. This new Orion turned and I saw those dimples; they weren't there before. I would swear on a stack of Bibles that this was not the same Orion who went behind the curtain for water. I can't explain it. I felt like crying. I was in shock. He did a few more songs, went back for more water, came back out and began another song. It was the first Orion again. Both are about the same height and weight and with the mask it's hard to tell—the lights and the identical costumes—the same everything, except for the dimples . . ."

"Elvis was very overweight. Orion, even *if* there are two of them, seems in good physical shape."

"You don't know Elvis. He was like a yo-yo with his weight. He could gain fast and lose fast. That's the truth. It's been over two years. Anyone can lose fifty pounds in that length of time. Elvis could do it in six weeks."

She honestly believed Elvis was alive. She actually took it for granted. Perhaps James Bacon was correct when he stated there were many who thought Elvis was alive? I honestly did not know what to think.

What I did know was that something out-of-the-ordinary was happening, and that certainly no other fictional book had begun such an incredible journey.

THE PLAN

While the novel ORION was experiencing an unusual life, the mystery surrounding the death of Elvis Presley created independent questions. From the moment fans saw him in the coffin, the questions began: who was in the coffin? Fans reported that it did not look like Elvis, that it looked more like a wax figure. "Since when did Elvis have a pug nose?" was one question. Others questioned the shape of the eyebrows, stating Elvis' were arched, while the figure in the coffin had straight brows. They questioned the shape of the chin, even the shape of the fingers.

Although picture-taking was not allowed, someone did take a picture and it appeared on the front page of THE NATIONAL ENQUIRER. I have a copy and I agree: it does not look like Elvis Presley.

Of course, in death, bodies often look different.

Even before Elvis was entombed in the white marble mausoleum in Forest Hill Cemetery, the cause of death was suspect. Although officially listed as "HCVD" associated with ASHD, or "hypertensive heart disease with coronary artery heart disease," no one believed it. Words such as "drugs," "cancer," were tauted. There was immediate talk of exhuming the body, that the autopsy report and Medical Examiner's report were inadequate, deceptive, and fraudulent.

According to Ken Lafolii's investigative report for THE WINDSOR STAR in Toronto, Canada, "Within a week of Elvis' funeral workmen at Forest Lawn Midtown disinterred the body of his mother late at night. They moved her from a hillside grave to a white marble crypt alongside Elvis, and when the municipal health department opened the next morning, cemetery officials were there to apply retroactively for a permit to move the body. The permit was granted. A few days later attorneys for the Presley estate applied for a zoning variance to allow the bodies of both Elvis and his mother to be moved, this time to a gravesite at Graceland.''

I understood, as do many biographers, that Gladys was moved prior to Elvis' funeral. This is a minor inconsistency. Ken Lefollii continues:

"Graceland was zoned R-1. In R-1 zones burials were not among the approved uses. Moreover, the act regulating burials said nothing about laying people down in residential areas. 'If it is not mentioned, it is not permitted,' said Dr. George Lovejoy, the director of the health department. 'But,' he added, 'it would be no problem to issue a health permit if the board of adjustment gave a variance.' The necessary documents were duly issued, and late one night the earthly remains of Elvis and his mother were quietly slipped from their crypts at Forest Hill and brought to Graceland where they now lie in a setting known as Meditation Gardens.''

Fans question when this moving of the bodies occurred? "In the months following Elvis' death there were always fans at Graceland and outside the crypt at Forest Hill—day and night. How could the bodies have been moved without anyone noticing?''

The moving of the bodies took place on October 2, 1977, approximately six weeks after the death of Elvis. The reason given for the move was said that Vernon feared Elvis' body would be kidnapped. Nearly two weeks after Elvis' funeral three men were arrested "attempting to steal the body of Elvis.'' This occurred on August 29, 1977. The men arrested said they did not want the body of Elvis but wanted to prove to the world that Elvis had *not died* and that there was no body in the crypt. This must have unnerved Vernon. Still, he waited over a full month before having the bodies moved. It was also during this period that talk abounded about exhuming the body because of the "cause of death'' controversy. Once the body was moved to Graceland the possibility of it being exhumed was drastically reduced. Plus the grounds of

Graceland are guarded by an electronic security system so sophisticated it could protect the greatest treasures of the world. Armed guards patrol the grounds twenty-four hours a day. And if an intruder miraculously did slip by the human and electronic detectors with the intent of kidnapping, it would be virtually impossible to reach a body protected by tons of granite slab, locked in a massive multi-ton sealed vault which holds the seamless coffin, a coffin that weighs nine hundred pounds.

The possibility of exhuming or kidnapping the body of Elvis Presley is unlikely.

The three charged with the kidnapping attempt were simply charged with trespassing and released on bond. Later Vernon dropped all charges. Why?

This in itself does not suggest a hoaxing of a death. After all, Elvis was a prisoner of fame while living. Since death his fame has soared beyond human expectations. Within twenty-four hours of his death RCA sold 20 million albums with an expected demand of 100 million. And according to a quote made by Geraldo Rivera on ABC's 20/20 in 1979, "Elvis Presley has sold over 800 million albums which means every family on the face of this planet could own an Elvis album."

Whatever the true figures are, it seems apparent that "in death" Elvis Presley is earning more than he did "in life."

What I find hard to rationalize is the spelling of Elvis' middle name on the gravestone in Meditation Gardens. Elvis' name has always been a source of interest particularly in those early years when he was an unknown. Those in power had often suggested Elvis change his name. After all, this was the era of the James Deans and Rock Hudsons. Could a name like Elvis Presley succeed?

Elvis defended his name for it was the name his parents chose. It was also in honor of his father Vernon whose middle name was "Elvis." He was proud of his name, of his heritage, and as we all know, had an extraordinary tie to both of his parents. To "fool around" with the name his parents chose was a subject not to breach. He was Elvis Presley and the world would have to accept him "as is."

He was also Elvis *Aron* Presley. Here lies the big question: Why did Vernon deliberately misspell Elvis' middle name on the grave, spelling it Elvis *Aaron* Presley?

In 1981 Albert Goldman in his bestseller ELVIS writes:

"Long before Gladys came to term she, became convinced that she was carrying twins. So strong was her belief that she and Vernon chose names for the unborn children. . . . To attain the mirror effect she was seeking she distorted the spelling of the twins' names, either deliberately or inadvertently through ignorance: 'Elvis Aron' was spelled with a single 'a' and 'Jessie Garon' with an 'o' instead of the customary 'i.' Further signs of ingenuity are the equivalent number of syllables in each name and the balance struct my matching one Old Testament name. Elvis or Garon. The final twist in the name knot attached the boys to their father by giving them all one name that rhymed: vis., Aron, Garon, Vernon. It was not, however, the connection with the father but the link with the other twin that was permanent. Gladys wanted to assure that throughout his entire future life Elvis Aron, for example, could never hear, speak or read his own name, without hearing in his mind its faint chiming echo—Jessie Garon.''

In Dave Marsh's pictorial book entitled ELVIS, on page 125, there is a full-blown shot of Elvis holding his army induction papers, dated December 18, 1957. Clearly it shows the legal name of Elvis **Aron** Presley. In another book, THE ELVIS CATALOG by Lee Cotten, there is a reproduced copy on page seventeen of Elvis' Memphis City School Diploma/L.C. Humes High School. It reads, ''Elvis **Aron** Presley.''

The Medical Examiner's Report and Death Certificate read, ''Elvis **Aron** Presley.''

The marriage certificate uniting him in marriage to Priscilla Ann Beaulieu reads, ''Elvis **Aron** Presley.''

The birth certificate that is sold at Graceland reads, ''Elvis *Aron* Presley.'' (One biographer states that on the original birth certificate the doctor who delivered Elvis mistakenly spelled Aron with a double ''a'' and that Elvis made sure the error was corrected.)

RCA, in all their promotions, list the name as Elvis **Aron** Presley.

All legal contracts spell the name as Elvis **Aron** Presley.

To further illustrate how important Elvis' name was to him I refer to Elaine Dundy's book ELVIS AND GLADYS:

"The naming of the Presley twins was highly significant. The firstborn was Jesse after Vernon's father. To the live child they gave the middle name **Aron**. To the dead Jesse, they gave the middle name Garon which rhymed with **Aron**."

Ms. Dundy interviewed many members of Elvis' family and was told, "Even as late as the age of thirteen, Elvis signed his name Elvis **aron** Presley with a small 'a.' According to handwriting expert Terence Gray this space for the missing 'G' of his brother's middle name indicates how strongly Elvis felt his brother's death."

Gladys in particular always wanted Elvis to look at his middle name "Aron" and know that it was "part of Garon." Goldman notes in his book ELVIS that in later years Elvis may have changed his middle name to the double "a." There is no evidence of this change and the opposite appears true. Elvis was too close to his parents to change a name they had given so much thought to. Secondly, he always expressed kinship to the dead twin and would not have marred the imagery. Third, what would be the point? If he balked about changing it when he was an unknown why would he change it once it became the most famous name in the world?

To prove my point why would the family of Elvis Presley (Vernon, Priscilla, Lisa) send out a thank-you card to the many fans which read:

The family of
Elvis **Aron** Presley
acknowledges with grateful
appreciation your kind expression
of sympathy

In a book ELVIS: WE LOVE YOU TENDER by the stepmother and stepbrothers of Elvis, they spell his middle name with the singular "a."

In ELVIS: WHAT HAPPENED? Red West, whose friendship with Elvis goes back to their Humes High School days, spells Elvis' middle name as "Aron" not "Aaron."

According to the Clerk of the Probate Court in Memphis, Tennessee on the Inventory of the Estate of Elvis A. Presley there is a company listed as "**Aron** Music, Inc., 75 shares," a company set up by Elvis, again using the correct spelling of his middle name.

And finally Elvis' own handwriting shows he used the Aron spelling (such as on the Elvis Aron Presley 8 LP Box Record Set . . .)

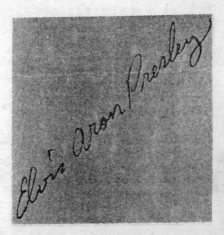

The placque on Elvis Presley Boulevard which welcomes visitors to Graceland reads: the home of Elvis **Aron** Presley.

There seems to be little argument that Elvis' middle name was **"Aron"** not "Aaron." And in many instances there is a great deal of story/history of *how* and *why* this unusual spelling occurred. Why then, would Vernon—who played such an important role in the naming of his only living son—change the spelling on the gravestone in Meditation Gardens? I noticed in the picture of the famous shrine that at the bottom right it states the inscription was ordered by Vernon Presley.

Elvis Aron Presley was the most well-known man to walk the planet. He was the idol of millions and millions of fans yet his final resting place—the immortal monument—has his name misspelled!

The Presleys are religious and also superstitious. If Elvis were not buried there it would be a bad omen to have his

In the Probate Court of Shelby County, Tennessee

No. A-655 R

Inventory   November 17, 1977

of the Estate of ELVIS A. PRESLEY, Deceased.

Your Executor would respectfully report that the

following assets belonging to said estate have come into his hands as follows, to-wit:

DATE (Values, where shown, are approximate values as of date of death):		
First Tennessee Bank-Savings Acct. #09-7067313	39	00
National Bank of Commerce-Savings Acct. #43-3-481-9	260	16
National Bank of Commerce-Savings Acct. #01-103-153-3	11,254	83
National Bank of Commerce-Savings Acct. #31-2-244-2	24,279	19
National Bank of Commerce-Checking Acct. #14-3891	57	57
National Bank of Commerce-Checking Acct. #14-3875	1,055,173	69
Del Webb Corporation - 696 shares		
Elvis Music, Inc. - 60 shares		
Whitehaven Music, Inc. - 60 shares		
Aron Music, Inc. - 75 shares		
Box Car Enterprises, Inc. - 75 shares		
Mr. Songman Music, Inc. - 75 shares		

name on the grave. (Many people even shy away from purchasing burial plots as preventive measures—a way of not fulfilling a prophecy.) If Elvis did not die on August 16, 1977, then it makes sense not to tempt fate by putting one's name on a tombstone if one is still alive—and you don't have to be superstititous to believe this. To misspell the name could be a method of saying, "It's not me."

Fate was not tempted. The gravestone reads:

Elvis **Aaron** Presley.

I have not been the only one to question why Vernon misspelled Elvis' middle name on the grave. A great majority of the fan newsletters and segments of the media have noticed the misspelling. What they cannot understand is *why* his name is misspelled? I would return that question and, without missing a beat, without exception, the answer was: "I think Elvis hoaxed his death," or "I don't think Elvis is buried there."

The majority though, as James Bacon underscored, feel that Elvis Aron Presley did not die. They also say they understand why. Some even said they predicted that a "faked death" would be his only way out.

Every day I receive more calls saying the same thing. Perhaps they want to believe. That's understandable. But so many? Many, too, have provided additional information. In fact there is a group who want to petition for the opening of the grave. They do not believe he died; therefore, they do not believe he is buried beneath the stone marker with the misspelled name.

It is difficult to write about such a confusing puzzle. Every turn of the page requires probing. Yet when the probing is done the puzzle remains incomplete.

By the various newspaper pictures I had noted immediately that Elvis' middle name was spelled incorrectly, but the year 1979 was still too early to see how this enigma fit into the larger picture. Later, after Vernon died, I would note something strange. And then when Elvis' grandmother Minnie Mae died, it would become even stranger.

It's quite clear without too much elaboration that Elvis Presley adored his mother Gladys Love Smith Presley. Everyone who knew him said he was devastated by her death, that he wanted to be with her, that he always said he would be

MISSISSIPPI STATE BOARD OF HEALTH

State File No. **1835**

1. PLACE OF BIRTH

County **Lee**

Tupelo

Registered No. **10**

1. Full name of child **Elvis Aaron Presley**

FATHER

Name **V. E. Presley**

Birthplace **Tupelo, Miss.**

MOTHER

Name **Gladys Smith**

Birthplace **Pontotoc, Miss.**

DEPARTMENT OF COMMERCE
Bureau of The Census

STANDARD CERTIFICATE OF LIVE BIRTH
STATE OF MISSISSIPPI

State File Number _____

Registrar's Number ____ **SOUVENIR**

FOR LIVE BIRTH ONLY — USE SPECIAL BLANK FOR RECORDING STILL BIRTH

1. PLACE OF BIRTH—
County _Lee_   City or Town _Tupelo_   or Street and No. _Dcdcdrille Rd_   Inside or Outside Corporate Limits? _Outside_

Hospital _at home_   or Rural Precinct ____

Mother's Stay Before Delivery—(s) In Hospital _at home_   (b) In the Community _Yes_

2. RESIDENCE OF MOTHER—
State _Miss_   County _Lee_   City or Town _Tupelo_   or Rural Precinct ____

3. FULL NAME OF CHILD _Elvis Aron Bradley_   4. DATE OF BIRTH _1-8-35_

5. **Boy**   6. Twin or Triplet? _Twin_   If born 1st, 2d, 3d   7. Number Months of Pregnancy _9_   9. Is Mother Married? _Yes_

FATHER OF CHILD
10. Full Name _Vernon Elvis Bradley_   11. Age at Time of this Birth _20_ yrs.
12. Color or Race _White_
13. Where _Mississippi_
14. Usual Occupation _Laborer_
16. Industry or Business ____

MOTHER OF CHILD
15. Full Maiden Name _Gladys Love_   17. Age at Time of this Birth _21_ yrs.
18. Color or Race _White_
18. Where _Mississippi_
19. Usual Occupation _Family Worker_
20. Industry or Business ____

7. CHILDREN BORN TO THIS MOTHER:
(a) How many other children of this mother are now living? _None_

22. Mother's Mailing Address for Registration Notice _Dcdcdrille Rd_

(b) How many other children were born alive but are now dead? _O_   (c) How many children were born dead? _1_

23. I hereby certify that I attended the birth of this child who was born alive at _M._ on the date above stated, and that the information given was furnished by _Vernon Bradley_ related to this child as _Father_

24. Date Rec'd. by Registrar _1-8-35_   (Signed) ____

4a. Signature of Registrar ____   Address ____

BOOK 248

405254

Marriage Certificate

No. A 175632

State of Nevada }
County of Clark. } ss.

This is to Certify that the undersigned JUSTICE DAVID ZENOFF

did on the 1st day of May A.D. 1967 join in lawful

Wedlock ELVIS ARON PRESLEY

of MEMPHIS State of TENNESSEE

and PRISCILLA ANN BEAULIEU

of SHELBY State of TENNESSEE

with their mutual consent, in the presence of Joe Esposito

and Marty Packer who were witnesses.

Recorded at the Request of David Zenoff

Date MAY 5 1967

In Book of Marriages, Clark County, Nevada,
Records, Paul E. Hern, Recorder.

Fee $1.00 Indexed _____ Deputy.

Richard Zenoff

JUSTICE, SUPREME COURT OF NEVADA
(Sign this in official capacity.)

Just as an aside, in crossword puzzles I've worked, Elvis' middle name is listed as **Aron**. For example:

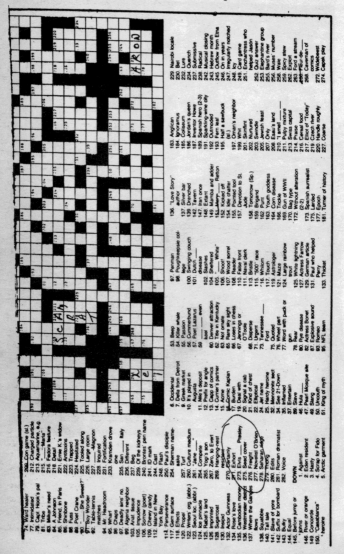

buried beside her. This truth is further accentuated by the fact that her body was moved from its first resting place at Forest Lawn Midtown to the white marble crypt at Forest Hill. This was done because, as the family stated, "burying Elvis in the open placed the body at risk from kidnappers." The crypt offered more security. Thus, Gladys was moved to lie beside Elvis, as Elvis often said was his wish.

Both the bodies of Elvis and Gladys were moved to Graceland when talk of exhuming the body of Elvis became a risk. Vernon placed them in the Meditation Gardens. Their stones lay side by side, as it should be. A few years later, Vernon died. Yet instead of placing Vernon's grave to the left of Elvis, so that Elvis would rest between his mother and father, Vernon's stone is between Elvis and his beloved mother. In other words, Elvis is buried *between* his father and his father's mother. *He is not next to Gladys*. This might seem insignificant in most cases. Not with Elvis. There was *no* reason to place anyone between Elvis and his mother. They were there first. To have it end up with Elvis between his father and grandmother is out-of-step with Elvis' posted desires—unless, of course, Elvis is not buried there. And if he is not buried there, neither is his father or mother.

"I believe Gladys is still in the crypt, as is Vernon and Minnie Mae," a friend of Elvis suggested. "I read in one magazine that the funeral home billed for only one moving of a body. The charge was over three thousand dollars, which must be the charge for moving Gladys from her original grave to the crypt. What about the charges for moving both bodies to Graceland? Were they actually moved? Was anyone moved . . . ?"

Somehow in all the confusion order reigned. Within hours Elvis' body was reportedly autopsied, taken to the Memphis Funeral Home, embalmed and returned to the mansion early the next day. Cause of death was from the beginning a mystery. Elvis was encased in a specially designed casket weighing 900 pounds which was flown in "overnight."

Other strange things were happening on August 16, 1977. Research of the various biographers shows that the Colonel, rather than returning immediately to Memphis, flew to New York where he met with the owner of a large merchandising firm. A deal was made to merchandise Elvis via the

Colonel's company, Boxcar Enterprises, owned 56 percent by the Colonel and 22 percent each by the Presley estate and the Colonel's assistant Tom Diskin, which means that of all the money that came in from nearly one hundred souvenirs marketed, Elvis received the least in revenues.

The Colonel was ready and was "taking care of business."

"It's still Elvis and the Colonel, but now it's Elvis and Vernon Presley and the Colonel," the Colonel told people on the telephone that week, according to Jerry Hopkins' ELVIS: THE FINAL YEARS. "Elvis *didn't* die. The body did. We're keeping up the good spirits. We're keeping Elvis alive. I talked to him *this morning* and he told me to carry on."

If it is discovered Elvis is still alive, at least the Colonel can have the last laugh: he can say, "I told you so. I told everyone he was alive. Said I talked to him. Only said the body was dead—didn't say *whose* body!"

(It might be well to note that the Colonel's stepson, Bobby Ross of Tampa, Florida ironically died quietly in 1977. Few people knew about this as so little is known about Colonel Tom Parker.)

As many Elvis historians have written, Elvis Presley was both a student and a believer in such concepts as parapsychology, numerology (the study of the occult significance of numbers), the occult, psychic phenomenon, mysticism and religions.

CHEIRO'S BOOK OF NUMBERS was a book Elvis consulted often. Family and friends attest to the fact Elvis consulted this book, planned his life and important activities according to it. In ELVIS: WE LOVE YOU TENDER, his family talks about his fascination with subjects of enlightenment.

> He studied the teachings of the Far East,
> particularly Buddhism.

> He delved into the theories surrounding
> meditation and yoga.

> He was fascinated with the inner workings
> of the human mind and the human body.

Medicine, psychology, parapsychology, and various philosophies intrigued him. Books that taught self-enlightenment became favorites.

He was interested in how human thought had developed over the centuries.

He studied the teachings of spiritualists, mystics, and psychics.

He looked into Scientology and the teachings of various gurus.

Beyond these interests Elvis questioned psychokinesis, mind control, telepathy, ESP and the connection between character and one's destiny.

The meaning of the vibration of numbers took on great significance. Goldman in his ELVIS told how Elvis consulted CHEIRO'S BOOK OF NUMBERS before deciding on an engagement date to Ginger Alden.

Very few books written about Elvis overlook his fascination with CHEIRO'S BOOK OF NUMBERS. It was usually beside him, beside his bed. He supposedly charted his concerts, his albums, and his life by the numbers. Carrying this book with him when he traveled, he was rarely without it. There are pictures of Elvis carrying it.

I stress CHEIRO'S BOOK OF NUMBERS for many reasons; if ELVIS were to plot his death, it would have to fit numerology and the sequence of numbers would have to have special meaning and a message for him alone.

Elvis always said he would die the same day as his mother and at the same age, 42. Many journalists to this day believe Gladys was 42 when she died on August 14, 1958. A close look at her grave reveals she was born April 25, 1912, which made her 46, not 42. Elvis knew her true age because several years after Gladys' death, Elvis added to her memorial stone the Star of David, which he wore with a cross around his neck. Elvis allowed this distortion of his mother's age. Perhaps because it better fit into his own plans. Although Elvis wore the Star of David and a cross around his neck, telling everyone that he did not want to avoid getting into Heaven on a technicality, he deliberately had it added to his mother's memorial stone. A close examination of Elvis' stone at Graceland bearing his mispelled name, shows only a cross and the TCB emblem, which means, "Taking Care of Business."

Why, when the Star of David was so important to him, does it *not* appear on his gravestone?

One would think that Vernon would not only spell his son's name correctly—the name he gave his son—but would honor Elvis' religious crossover. He knew of Elvis' wishes. They certainly came across loud and clear. Thus again, we have another interesting enigma about the gravestone.

If Elvis were to choose a date to "leave," he would definitely check CHEIRO's. Twenty-four is the ideal vibration. It means fortunate, promises assistance and association "to those of rank and position" and is the most favorable number when it comes out in relation to such plans.

Elvis was also aware of the power of threes. It is said to have the ideal vibration, a date would have to work perfectly at least three times. In this case it would have to come out to 24. There is a great deal of significance to the date August 16, 1977. In numerology that means the 8th month, 16th day, 1977 year. Add 8 plus 16 plus 1977 and you come up with the number 2001.

One of the most important numbers in the life of Elvis was 2001. It was his theme song (from 2001: SPACE ODYSSEY, or Thus Spake Zarathustra).

To test the importance of that date and number further and the perfect number 24, we find that only August 16, 1977 would have worked. Elvis may have wanted to use August 14, the date of Gladys' departure, but he couldn't work out the three 24's he needed. He had to choose the 16th. And since 2001 was a pivotal starting point, it worked. Consider August 16, which is the eighth month and sixteenth day, totaling 24. When the number 1977 is added, it also totals 24. Furthermore, 1977 subtracted from the key number 2001 yields the third 24 needed to make the perfect plan work. Elvis could have further verified this date by taking the year of his birth, 1935, add to it the age chosen for death, 42, added with the 8th month and 16th day and again come up with the coveted 2001. (1935 plus 42 plus 8 plus 16 equals 2001.)

Elvis was pleased to discover that although the number eight was his numerical vibration, his name number was a nine, as was the name number of Jesus. (Each letter of a name has its own number. It's the combination of these numbers which broken down give you your name number.)

The film 2001: SPACE ODYSSEY from which Elvis chose his theme song concerns the cosmic order of man through space and time, man's infinite and glorious immortality inside a spacecraft named Orion. If Elvis deliberately chose this date, then it's interesting to note that in the film it is "in the toilet" where the supreme character or hero executed his plans for immortality. Recall that Elvis' body was found in his bathroom. 2001 is about illusion and the metaphysical. I find this even more intriguing when one considers the emergence of a singer named Orion—two masked illusions?

In Priscilla Presley's book ELVIS AND ME, she speaks about Elvis' fascination with CHEIRO'S BOOK OF NUMBERS. Elvis was a number eight which is described as one who is alone at heart, who often hides feelings but in the end does as he pleases. Priscilla was afraid that her personality traits and characteristics would not be in harmony with Elvis. But after Elvis added up her birthday numbers she was relieved to find she was compatible after all.

Later she describes an incident that took place a few months prior to August of 1977. Both she and Lisa were at the mansion. Elvis had cancelled a tour due to illness. Elvis called her up to his bedroom in order to read her something important from CHEIRO'S BOOK OF NUMBERS.

Apparently Elvis was deeply intent on finding his place in the universe. Many, including Priscilla, state Elvis had not discovered his purpose in life. Priscilla stated in one interview Elvis would have been happy on a small farm someplace, out of the limelight. He told a news reporter that he wished he could be like him—that he wished he could walk around like an ordinary person. His stepmother said he would have been happy as a doctor. Others stated Elvis' true calling was the ministry. Whatever Elvis was searching for, it is apparent he wanted to heal, to help, to give, which explains his legendary generosity.

Elvis *was* a man in search. Part of this search apparently rested within the pages of a book of numbers. Perhaps there Elvis would find the answer. Priscilla does not explain *what* it was Elvis wanted her to read. However, it had to hold importance. Priscilla must have been of importance to Elvis as he shared his search. *What* was it in CHEIRO'S that held significance? And did it have anything to do with what was to come?

Later she says something very interesting. Remember, Elvis never travelled or went anywhere without CHEIRO'S BOOK OF NUMBERS. He hand-carried it. He read it on the airplane, kept it beside him in hotel rooms, hospital rooms, his bedroom.

Yet—hours after death . . .

When Priscilla went up to Elvis' bedroom, she found something very strange: his nightstand was **bare of books.**

(In the Inventory of the Estate report there is no mention of CHEIRO'S, or the Bible or any book.)

What happened to CHEIRO'S BOOK OF NUMBERS? Had he already packed it away? We know Elvis was not reading that particular book the day he "died." If he had hoaxed his death, he would have certainly "packed CHEIRO'S and his Bible." In all the confusion, no one would notice. Yet the other side of the coin is if Elvis did indeed die, why, in all the confusion and sorrow, would anyone pack away these books just hours after the death?

Perhaps Elvis did take them with him.

. . . not to the other side though.

THE TRUTH

I have recieved several copies of the certificate of death
from the office of the Medical Examiner. This further compli-
cates matters. The name is spelled correctly: Elvis **Aron.** One
variation of the same copy lists the body weight at 170
pounds. Elvis was said to be around 250 pounds at the time
of "death." Another copy has the weight missing. At 170 he
would have looked like the old Adonis he once was. Since I
was not the only person with a copy of this report, I wondered about the weight. Whose weight was listed? Whose
body was weighed? I refer again to columnist James Bacon,
who wrote about this controversial oddity:

"One controversy that refuses to die is whether Elvis
Presley really did die. You would be amazed at how many
people think Elvis still lives. Apropos of all the controversy, I have obtained a copy of Elvis' death report. It
only seems to make things worse.

The report of the county medical examiner in Memphis,
Tenn., lists Elvis' weight as 170 pounds. A call to the
examiner's office reports that all corpses are weighed and
any variation would depend upon how much food the dead
man had in his stomach when found.
Everyone I have talked to who saw Elvis in those last days
put his weight at well over 200 pounds. One even had it as
high as 250.

It also lists that family consent was required for an autopsy. Usually when someone is found dead unattended an autopsy is automatic. At least, it was when I was a police reporter.

Cause of death is listed as hypertensive cardiac vascular disease with arterial scleratic heart disease. It also states that Elvis had been playing racquetball in the early morning of the day he died.   .

For someone with that heart condition, racquetball seems like a strange game to play.

He was last seen alive at 8 a.m. and his body was discovered by his girlfriend, Ginger Alden at 2 p.m. the same day.

I average about two or three calls a day from all over the country from people who sound like ordinary Elvis fans. They all believe Elvis faked his own death so he could live a normal life.
Weird.''

This same report was shown visually by Geraldo Rivera on ABC's 20/20 entitled THE COVER-UP IN THE DEATH OF ELVIS PRESLEY in 1979. This leads me to believe the certificate with the 170 pound weight may be the earlier of the two because both James Bacon and 20/20 are reputable sources and would have checked it out. However in 1978 Ken Lefolii wrote an article for THE WINDSOR STAR in Toronto concerning the Medical Examiner's report:

''My copy was handed to me in the office of Dr. Dan Warlick, and when I had glanced at it long enough to see how little it said I asked him if he had examined the body itself.
    'Of course,' he said, bridling a little. 'I am the chief medical investigator in his jurisdiction.'
    In that case, could he tell me some of the things the official report had left out? To begin with the simplest, why was the space after Weight left blank, and how much did the dead man weigh?

'Anything that's not on that form is the private property of the Presley family,' he said. 'They signed the autopsy request. Under Tennessee law, that means they own the results. And they're locked in the vault at Baptist Memorial.'

'Even his weight?'

'Even his weight,' he said, and smiled.''

Although it is not clear which report was first, it is clear that something *is* wrong with the weight. I also find it strange that there are two birth certificates and now two death certificates, if there is a death certificate at all. Both of these certificates bear the date October 20, 1977 which is two months after August 16, 1977. A death certificate is issued almost immediately so that family can collect insurance. Upon checking up on still another enigma I was told that the original death certificate had disappeared and this disappearance was not noted until October 20th when a new one was issued. It has also been reported that no insurance was collected.

There are other inconsistencies:

The Medical Examiner's report states the body was found ''unclothed.'' Yet in all the books I've read it states Elvis was found wearing pajamas although the color of these pajamas differs. In ELVIS: WE LOVE YOU TENDER it says Elvis was found ''wearing a pair of blue cotton pajamas.'' The book ELVIS states Elvis was ''clothed in pajamas—a yellow top and blue bottoms.'' A third book says Elvis was ''wearing black pajamas.''

Did anyone actually see the body of Elvis?

ELVIS: WE LOVE YOU TENDER talks about Elvis being alone in his bathroom where he ''dropped his book, kneeled over onto his face.'' That book quotes Ginger Alden as having opened the door and found Elvis ''sprawled across the floor.'' This sighting changes somewhat in the book ELVIS in regards to Ginger's discovery of the body. ''Finally, she opened the door and peeped inside. What she saw was Elvis doubled up face down on the floor, with his buttocks elevated, in the fetal position. Clearly, he had been sitting in the black leather and chrome chair reading and had toppled forward onto the floor. The book was still lying on the chair.''

How could Elvis be both doubled up and sprawled? How could he have been reading a book, toppled forward and then that same book is found lying on the chair? He would either have been reading the book by sitting on it or having fallen forward with chest pains, would have been meticulous enough to, in the throes of a heart attack, placed the fallen book on the chair.

Both Albert Goldman in ELVIS and David Stanley say that it was the SHROUD OF TURIN by Ian Wilson, a book about Jesus and the evolution of Christian theology that Larry Geller had given Elvis as a present, as the book Elvis had been reading at the time of death. I purchased this book and discovered it was not copyrighted until 1978, a year **after** Elvis' death.

Ginger Alden has also stated that the thought of Elvis being dead never entered her mind. Albert Goldman described a scene in ELVIS whereby Joe Esposito was called. When he turned Elvis over on his back he heard a sighing sound, convincing him that Elvis was still breathing. Yet the Medical Examiner's report states the body was found dead and rigor mortis had set in.

All of the books seem to disagree on what was being done for Elvis. Some say tubes went down the throat into the lungs to administer air directly. An intracardiac injection of adrenalin is usually pumped directly into the heart, and catheters can be run into the arms through which drugs can be run to increase blood pressure.

Elvis' stepbrother, David Stanley, recalls seeing no injections or catheters.

If all else fails, there is the cardioverter, two powerful electrodes to opposite sides of the heart sending a jolt of electricity that can resynchronize the electrical impulses of the heart.

That was not attempted. At least not at the house.

The two paramedics called to the scene have stated they did not recognize the body as that of Elvis Presley.

When Ken Lefolii (THE WINDSOR STAR, Toronto) looked at the homicide report on Elvis Presley, he saw the following:

Offense Report No. 2793
Subject: Presley, Elvis
Offense: DOA
The above subject was brought to the Baptist Hospital after being found unconscious in the upstairs bedroom of his

70

home. The subject was transported by fire department ambulance and was DOA at the hospital. Homicide and the medical examiner did make the scene at the hospital and at 3764 Elvis Presley Boulevard.

Status: Pending

Reporting Officer: Sgt. R. E. Millican

When Mr. Lefolii asked to see the rest of the report he was told it was classified confidential. The net result of his report was that there was a "conspiracy of silence" surrounding the death of Elvis Presley.

The Medical Examiner's report states that Elvis was last seen alive at 8:00 A.M., although Ginger Alden has stated in some books that it was 9:00 A.M. Moot point, perhaps, but it is another inconsistency. Ginger stated she discovered the body around 2 P.M. which is consistent with the Medical Examiner's report listed under "Discovery, 1400." Yet in another interview which appeared in US MAGAZINE dated August 24, 1984 Ginger Alden says she found the body at 12:30 P.M., *not* 2 P.M.

According to this report it appears that although the body was discovered at 1400 there is a time lapse of an hour and a half until police were notified at 1530 and the medical examiner notified at 1600. It also reads that Elvis was pronounced dead at 1530. If it's true that Elvis was DOA and rigor mortis had set in, why so long in pronouncing him dead? If the truth is that Elvis was found unconscious then how could rigor mortis have set in? Why does the homicide report state Elvis was found unconscious while the medical examiner's report states he was found dead? If he was found dead why would it take so long for the pronouncement?

The Medical Examiner's report also states that resuscitation was attempted. (On a dead body where rigor mortis had set in?)

"Family consent signed for autopsy to be performed at BMH" (Baptist Memorial Hospital): As James Bacon pointed out, when a body is found unattended an autopsy is automatic. This is true in the state of Tennessee. However, when ABC tried to obtain a copy of the autopsy report a Memphis court ruled that since the autopsy was requested by the family and not the county it was protected by the privacy rule for

71

fifty years. We have the answer as to why the autopsy was consented to by family members.

It is reasonable to assume that these same "family" members must have known beforehand about this legal "out" since the body was supposedly autopsied immediately. Since Priscilla has said she was in California and Lisa, although at the mansion, was only nine years old, it must have been Vernon who signed the autopsy consent papers. I find it odd that Vernon would have been so legally informed within hours of losing his only son and odder still, that Vernon was not even at the hospital when the pronouncement and autopsy were done!

From what I've learned, Vernon was not that educated.

During the 20/20 hour show on the cover-up, Geraldo Rivera pointed out that the contents of Elvis' stomach had been destroyed **before** the autopsy and that the police had closed the case the night of the death. There are those who argue the reason autopsy remains were destroyed and the report sealed is because the family did not want the world to know that Elvis misused drugs. The book ELVIS: WHAT HAPPENED? contained page after page of Elvis' drug misuse. To plan an elaborate cover-up on an image that had been publically smeared, seems to be a case of "locking-the-barn-after-the-horse-has-been-stolen" rationale. Obviously the fans were sticking by their idol no matter what, as demonstrated by the massive crowds outside Graceland.

Did all of this mean Elvis was alive? No. Perhaps the body weight was either left out or distorted because Vernon wanted the world to think his son was still young and thin, despite the fact he was grossly overweight, as film and pictures show. In fact, he was grossly overweight only hours before. Therefore no one would have been fooled. So why?

If we're to believe that there were multiple plots for a multiple of reasons such as the misspelling of the name on the grave because Elvis is elsewhere, or the contents destroyed and the Medical Examiner's report altered because of image, we're still stuck with the question as to who orchestrated the cover-up? Vernon was suffering from heart trouble and in ill health. He doesn't strike me as the sort to go to such extremes.

The one person smart and bold enough to do this might be Elvis himself. He knew all about pharmaceuticals; he knew about illusion. He studied mysticism. He often visited the Memphis Funeral Home late at night, taking friends with him. Not only did he know about embalming, about how long a body would take to deteriorate, but he also knew which kind of drugs would intermingle safely with another. He could have taken one or more drugs to induce a coma-like state, but he would have needed the assistance of several friends, a doctor and even, perhaps, the Colonel.

Elvis knew the laws of fasting: in fasting toxins are released quicker from the body. Thus, if one were to tempt fate by taking enough drugs to put one in a temporary catatonic state, it would be wise to have that same body in a state of fasting so that the toxins could be eliminated as quickly as possible. Jerry Hopkins writes in ELVIS: THE FINAL YEARS:

"On August 14 he started a fast, something he often did to lose weight quickly before going on tour. Oddly, he didn't take any Ionamin, the appetite suppressant that he had favored for so long. Perhaps he believed the racquetball and fasting were enough. Besides, what difference did it really make? At 250 pounds he was grossly overweight and in two days how much could he lose? Five pounds? Be truthful, how good could he look in his bathroom mirror at 245? He'd still have sixty pounds he didn't want to see."

This fasting of August 14th appears in other books. What universally is questioned is why? There was no way Elvis could have lost weight for the tour which was to begin on August 16th. And why not the usual Ionamin? Could it be that Ionamin would have an adverse reaction if mixed with something else—something else that could give the appearance of death?

Elvis knew his drugs.

"Elvis consulted the big, thick Merck manual regularly, checking recommended dosages and side effects," Jerry Hopkins states.

Sonny West says in ELVIS: WHAT HAPPENED?, "He knows what pill to mix with another pill. He knows the dosages and the exact result. Sometimes he has miscalculated and had bad effects, but most of the time he knows what he is doing . . . He has got medical directories on the pills and he knows the color codes. Show him a pill or tell him its color on the capsule, and he can identify it in a second.''

The end analysis is that Elvis Presley was last seen alive somewhere between eight in the morning and as late as ten in the morning, and his body was discovered somewhere between 12:30 P.M. and 2:00 P.M. By all accounts he had an active day and evening and had had active days prior since Lisa Marie was visiting—taking Lisa and her friends to Libertyland Amusement Park and movies. Even his last day was busy watching television, reading, going to the dentist, staying up all night, playing racquetball, kidding and being generally in good spirits. No one who saw him during those last hours reported that he seemed ''drugged'' or unable to perform. In fact some say he played a rigorous game of racquetball, even worked out a bit. He seemed excited about what was supposed to happen on the 16th.

When 20/20 did their investigative piece on the cover-up, they concurred that the last 12 hours of Elvis' life were busy.

None of the doctors at Baptist Memorial Hospital would talk to 20/20 about the autopsy results and ABC sued Shelby County Medical Examiner, Dr. Jerry C. Francisco and Shelby County. It was revealed that ''no gross evidence of a heart attack or an irregularity in heartbeat was apparent enough to cause death.''

It was also discovered that in 1966 and shortly before August 16, 1977, Elvis underwent annual physicals (required by Lloyds of London, the insurance firm) and, according to sources he passed both with flying colors—there was no sign of heart disease.

Despite these medical statements, cause of death is listed on the Medical Examiner's report as heart problems.

The analyzation of stomach contents is vital in pin-pointing cause of death. Yet in the case of Elvis Presley stomach contents were destroyed ''without ever being analyzed.'' Crucial evidence was deliberately destroyed. Why?

Reports vary as to the different prescribed drugs for Elvis— some say eleven, others fourteen. These drugs were kept in the resident nurse's trailer. She reported that she only sent up Valium.

Geraldo Rivera and 20/20 ended the hour-long show with the statement that it was the worst medical investigation ever made in this century and that no real medical effort was made to determine the cause of death of Elvis Presley. These are some of the items 20/20 pointed out:

Item #1: No real police investigation was ever made and at nine in the evening of the death, before it was medically or scientifically possible to determine why and how Elvis Presley died, the Memphis Police considered this case closed.*

Item #2: Dr. Jerry Francisco said a search was made at Graceland for drugs and there were not any. However, a man who worked for Francisco stated no search was made of the resident nurse's trailor where all drugs were kept.

Item #3: Stomach contents were destroyed without ever having been analyzed.

Item #4: There was never—ever—a Coroner's Inquest.

Item #5: The Shelby County District Attorney was never officially notified to determine if there were any violations of criminal law.

Item #6: No attempts were ever made—even after the toxicology reports—to find out where Elvis had been getting all the drugs listed.

Item #7: All the photographs taken at the death scene, all notes of the Medical Examiner's investigation, all of the toxicology reports "allegedly" prepared by the Medical Examiner are missing from the official files.**

Item #8: Officials of the county government believe there has been a cover-up.***

---

*According to another report it was at eight ten when the body was "removed from Baptist Memorial and taken to the Memphis Funeral Home" which was owned by a friend of the family. Elvis was a patron of the Memphis Police Department. He wore its badges, had police uniforms, wanted to be a police officer. He often went out on drug busts in disguise.

**There is very little evidence to prove Elvis Presley died. *All* documentation is missing or destroyed.

***These same officials have stated that the truth be brought out, that the public should not be deceived any longer.

Both Dr. Nichopoulos and Dr. Francisco's name appear on the Medical Examiner's report. Elvis was very close to his personal physician known as "Dr. Nick." Elvis loved the man, and Dr. Nick loved Elvis. Would Dr. Nick have agreed to help Elvis in his escape to freedom?

(Ironically in my novel ORION, written long before Dr. Nick faced criminal charges, I had a doctor involved in the hoaxing of the death of a superstar singer.)

It is reported Dr. Nichopolous was in serious financial trouble in the seventies. A 5.5 million dollar professional building he had invested in was only one-third occupied. In 1975 he had borrowed $200,000 from Elvis and two years later, another $55,000. He was deeply indebted to Elvis Presley—in fact much of his professional income may have depended on Elvis and Elvis' family and friends. He also loved Elvis like a son. I find it easier to believe he would have helped Elvis "escape" rather than kill Elvis with pills.

I am not alone in this belief.

Beyond the 20/20 investigation I read another report in a newspaper which said, "After Elvis Presley purportedly died, Dr. Jerry Francisco said he performed an autopsy. He stated that cardiac arrhythmia was the cause of death. Maurice Elliott, the vice president of Baptist Memorial Hospital has been quoted in various publications stating that 'Elvis Presley's vital organs were never returned to his body . . . Elvis was buried without them.' "

Why?

Or, was there an autopsy? And if there was, on *whose* body was it done?

Ginger Alden is also quoted as stating that when she found Elvis, she reached down and touched him and he was "cold as ice" which she did not find unusual and instead found it typical since Elvis preferred rooms where the temperature had been forced down twenty degrees by a powerful air conditioner. She, in fact, states that she thought he was alive. My point is that there are many different stories about the condition of the body, the times involved, whether he was dead or alive, whether rigor mortis had set in or not, the color of his pajamas, whether he was wearing them or not, the title of the book he was reading, where the book was found, the position of the body, or, for that matter, whether the body that was discovered was really Elvis. Even as I compile this material, I find more than one side to the same coin, more than one answer. What is obvious is that there is enormous intrigue, controversy and cover-up.

Stories continually change. Those who questioned openly in 1977 now refuse to talk. For instance the following excerpt from US MAGAZINE's August 24, 1987 issue emphasized:

> "When he's told that a reporter wants to talk about Elvis, Dr. Vasco Smith comes right to the phone. 'Well, to tell you the truth, I was always a jazz fan,' drawls the longtime Memphis physician. 'So I wasn't all that familiar with his music.'
>
> 'Okay, fine—but Dr. Smith, weren't you a county commissioner at the time of Elvis' death and autopsy?'
>
> 'Oh,' he says quietly. 'Well, that's all over with. I don't have anything to say about that anymore.'
>
> 'But several years ago, you did tell a nationwide TV audience that you thought there'd been a cover-up . . .'
>
> 'I really don't have any comment.' "

Many of Elvis' fans and national fan clubs have telephoned or written me concerning ORION and concerning their belief that Elvis may have hoaxed his death. One club in particular which puts out a quarterly news magazine, THE ELVIS SPECIAL, has been most helpful. Maria Columbus, its co-president, has supplied me with valuable information. Independently they have been investigating the death of Elvis. They've also responded to the 20/20 investigation with the following:

> Elvis was in pain. He had to take medication. Elvis had a vast library of medical texts. He knew exactly what he was doing. He knew his medicine. (The migraine headaches alone due to the glaucoma would be enough to warrant medication.)

Elvis' generosity is being turned into selfishness—given only to receive favors of drugs and women.

It is alleged that Elvis was "shooting up." Yet why were there no needle marks, nor were his nasal membranes burned out had he been "sniffing."

How could Elvis have consumed thousands of pills and still perform such grueling tour schedules, especially in the past two years? His body would have been incapacitated.

Elvis took prescription drugs for a variety of problems: twisted colon, glaucoma, high blood pressure . . .

It is alleged that Elvis was on uppers much of the time yet every fan knows that Elvis was a very hyper person, with enormous amounts of nervous energy. Uppers would only aggravate that condition.

If Elvis had taken as much medicine as alleged, how did he manage to play racquetball for hours? Large doses would have knocked him out flat.

It is apparent that the fans give Elvis the benefit of the doubt. It is true they do not want Elvis' image destroyed as stated in THE ELVIS SPECIAL, "We were the ones who watched Elvis day after day. We were the ones who followed Elvis for twenty-five years. We were the ones who went on the tours, to the concerts. We were the ones who saw the entire truth. We lived through it, not 20/20."

Regardless of who has the complete truth, it is the fans who played a major role in the destiny of Elvis Presley. And it is many of these same fans who believe Elvis Presley never died on August 16, 1977. 20/20 asked questions. And so do they. The two variations of the same death certificate: one shows the body weighed 170 pounds. The other has the body weight blank. In both cases, this raises the same question: who was buried? Was anyone buried?

Note the date of the report: October 20, 1977. Where is the original? Is there an original?

234

Death Certificate

Case No. 77-1944

REPORT OF INVESTIGATION BY COUNTY MEDICAL EXAMINER

NAME: Elvis Presley   COLOR: W   SEX: M   AGE: 42   OCCUPATION: Entertainer

DISPOSITION OF CASE

PROBABLE CAUSE OF DEATH

HCVD

ASHD

PERSONAL HISTORY

CIRCUMSTANCES OF DEATH

NARRATIVE SUMMARY OF CIRCUMSTANCES SURROUNDING DEATH:

Jan 17, 1944

OFFICE OF THE

REPORT OF INVESTIGATION BY COUNTY MEDICAL EXAMINER

DECEDENT Elvis Presley — No. M.E. 77 vol. 42

HOME ADDRESS 3754 Elvis Presley Blvd.

TYPE OF DEATH: Violent ☐ Casualty ☐ Sudden ☐ Sudden, when a private physician ☐ Found Dead ☒ in Presence ☐ Accidental, natural or unattended ☐ Could not

Contacts

If Motor Vehicle Accident Driver ☐ Passenger ☐ Pedestrian ☐ Unknown ☐

Residence or Rest: Clothed ☐ Unclothed ☐ Partly Clothed ☐ Covered ☐ Yes ☐ No ☐

Inches ___ New Born ___ Scratches ___ Lived ___ Body Temp. Position ___ Date and Time

Weight 170 lbs. ___ Liver ☐ Lime Color ☐ Found ☐ Fixed ☐ Not Found ☐

Race: Yes ☐ No ☐

Marks and Wounds

DISPOSITION OF CASE
Did a medical examiner view it ☐
Autopsy requested Yes ☐ No ☐
Autopsy refused Yes ☐ No ☐
Pathologist ☐

NUMBER OF DEATH
(Check one only)
Accident ☐ Natural ☐
Suicide ☐ Undetermined ☐
Homicide ☐ Pending ☐

PROBABLE CAUSE OF DEATH

HCVD
ASHD

I hereby declare that after viewing the body ...
the cause of death in accordance with Section ... Tennessee Code ...
... of my knowledge and belief.

CIRCUMSTANCES OF DEATH

NARRATIVE SUMMARY OF CIRCUMSTANCES SURROUNDING DEATH:

"I Will Be Home Again"
—Elvis Presley Song—1960

ANOTHER ORION?

The name change on the grave continued to disturb me as well as the results of the 20/20 investigation. There were too many unanswered questions regarding the death of Elvis Presley. Bits of information were appearing randomly across the country from independent writers. Not all believed Elvis was alive. Most believed there was a cover-up. Fan newsletters continued to mention various oddities:

Why had Elvis bid "adios" at his final concert—something he had never done before.

Why had Elvis ordered no new costumes for his multi-city concert tour which he was leaving for on August 16, 1977?

There is no doubt Elvis was terribly overweight. On his last tour Elvis found that only two of the many costumes he owned fit. He had to alternate wearing them. Frenzied staff made efforts to have them cleaned between shows.

One of the two costumes that fit, he finally split. Why didn't he have new costumes made? And why would he, only six weeks later, plan another concert tour and not have any costumes? Is it because he knew he wouldn't need them?

Rick Stanley in ELVIS: WE LOVE YOU TENDER also speaks of the last tour (May/June, 1977), how "different" it was, how sad Elvis seemed, how Elvis began to use the song

MY WAY ("and now the end is near") at the close of the shows. During one of the last shows, Elvis frowned sadly and turned to Rick, his stepbrother, and said, "Know what, Rick? I may not look too good tonight . . . but I'll look good in my coffin."

"And with that," Rick writes, "Elvis Presley stepped out to face America for the last time."

Why had RCA already had an abundance of Elvis albums in the record stores?
Why had the presses been working day and night?

Elvis' last concert was on June 26, 1977 in Indianapolis—coincidentally where the RCA plant is.

Why had Elvis "cleaned house," getting rid of old friends and associates such as Red and Sonny West and Dave Hebler?

Why were there an abundance of tee-shirts and souvenirs ready to sell to the fans immediately after the death was announced?

Why hadn't Elvis had his hair and sideburns dyed as he usually did before going on tour?

Those who saw Elvis on the 15th and 16th say his side-burns were down to his chin and grey was showing. Yet Larry Geller, Elvis' psychic-hairdresser, is quoted in the book ELVIS that a short time prior to the body of Elvis being viewed he had to glue down a "sideburn that had come loose." If Elvis' sideburns were long, why would they have been shaved off and then fake sideburns glued on? This gives credibility to the fact that most fans who viewed the body say it was not Elvis but was instead a wax dummy.

ROUSTABOUT, a fan newsletter, talks about Elvis having told his aunt that fans at concerts never listened to what he was saying. "Elvis all but told us what he intended to do, downright bold about it. The clincher being the line in the song HURT where he states fans have not heard a word he

82

said. Look at how many think he's dead, without one shred of decent evidence."

I found the fans' questions intriguing but I saw no reason to do my own investigation. I was more concerned with trying to figure out the existence of the singer Orion and getting my novel to the public. I was also involved with another New York agent (having turned down William Morris) plus I was working with an independent publisher on the release of a Collector's Edition.

Roz Targ, a literary agent, telephoned as soon as she read ORION. "My dear, ORION is marvelous. It's a snowy day in New York and I can't put the book down . . ."

We talked about ORION; she wanted to handle it. I told her "I did not want to sign a three-year exclusive." I believe I kept William Morris' interest in the book out of the conversation. In regards to my hesitation about a three-year exclusive Roz assured, "If I can't sell ORION within 90 days, I wouldn't want to handle it."

Roz delivered what she promised. She sold ORION to Simon and Schuster's Pocket Books division for $60,000. There was every reason to believe the publisher would stand publically behind the book, and originally I am convinced that was their plan. By now David Dortort, creator/producer of TV's BONANZA, expressed interest in making ORION into a movie in conjunction with Avrum Fine of FILM AMERICA.

I was excited over the attention ORION was receiving. In a conversation with Roz, she mentioned she had shown ORION to Ballantine as well. I mentioned this to several people in Nashville. I was pleased that at last things were going well. Not long after I received a very strange late night telephone call. The voice over the telephone identified himself as Orion. By now I was wondering about *which* voice could be calling, if indeed there were two voices? All I could do was listen closely. Basically he began the conversation by stammering, "I,ah, heard something about your selling the book to,ah, Ballantine."

At the time the late night telephone call came I had not yet signed with Simon and Schuster. I explained that several publishers were looking at it, but nothing had been decided.

Orion continued. "I don't think you should let Ballantine

publish ORION. I mean, you said it right. Elvis is like Orion.''

I reminded this mystery voice that ORION was a novel and thus fiction. ''I'm glad you like the book, but it really isn't about Elvis; I never knew Elvis, never was around him. I truly made everything up.'' Even the ending I wanted to add. ''Everything is fiction,'' and so are you I also wanted to stress.

''Then I don't know how you knew so much,'' the voice insisted. ''Maybe I do understand, though. I understand those things.''

''What things?''

''What I'm trying to say is that Ballantine knows that ELVIS: WHAT HAPPENED? is not the truth. But they published it. You shouldn't let them have ORION. I don't think it's right.''

''What isn't true?''

''A lot of it. Especially the drug thing. And that part about Elvis throwing a pool cue at a young lady, stabbing her in the chest. Those boys who wrote it said Elvis did it deliberately. That's not the truth and they know it. Elvis wasn't playing good, got mad and turned and threw the cue. He wasn't aiming. It was an accident. It's not good to have a temper but it was an accident. That's the truth. Those boys told it wrong. It's simply not true,'' he repeated.

The voice appeared sincerely upset. What I couldn't understand was why? Orion was a man named Jimmy Ellis; why would he take what happened to Elvis so personally? And how would he know the true story? Was he a friend of Elvis? Was he a front? Or was it possible that the voice over the telephone was not Jimmy Ellis/Orion? Again, I felt victimized and toyed with.

I couldn't understand the call so I telephoned Cindy Baum, the niece of David Dortort. It was in the middle of the night but I was upset and curious. She didn't know what to make of it either.

I also told Carole Halupke of the call. She agreed that the text of the conversation was very strange. Sometime later there was another Orion concert with bodyguards, fantastic costumes, and mystery. I was allowed backstage; I took a friend, Mary Beth Danielski. By this time I was trying to have as much as possible witnessed. During the conversation with Orion I said, "By the way. You don't have to worry about my going with Ballantine. My agent placed it with another publisher."

Orion stared at me perplexed. "Ballantine? I don't know what you're talking about?"

Having told Mary Beth about the telephone call, we stared at each other in shock. Orion knew *nothing* about the conversation in question. How could that be possible? I had no idea who put out ELVIS: WHAT HAPPENED? That information came from the voice-over-the-telephone, a voice that sounded identical to Elvis Presley. Yet Orion sounded like Elvis Presley. I found it hard to believe the unbelievable. Carole and I discussed the possibility that there might be two Orions but then usually rationalized, "No, that's too far-fetched."

Except . . .

Another very late telephone call. Same voice. This time my son Christopher, then a teenager, answered. The voice asked Chris if he could speak "to your mama."

I was lying on the couch reading. "It's for you, Mom," Chris announced.

"Who is it?" I asked annoyed, thinking it was rather late for calls.

"Who's calling?" Chris asked.

Chris related the following. "There was a long pause, and then the man said, 'Ah, tell her it's Orion.' "

Chris became excited. He had heard enough conversations around the house about the possibility of there being two Orions, and that one of the two might possibly be Elvis. When Chris exclaimed, "Orion!" with so much awe, Chris says the voice laughed and then began asking him questions about himself. He wanted to know Chris' age, what he liked to do. The subject of horseback riding came into the conversation as did hunting. Chris liked hunting squirrels but the voice said he disliked killing animals.

"But you like to ride horses?" the voice asked. Chris said he did and for about five minutes horses became part of their conversation, with his telling Chris he had a horse farm near Macon and that maybe someday Chris could go riding with him, "if everything turned out."

Finally the telephone was turned over to me. At first

there seemed no particular reason for the call. I listened closely wondering which Orion was calling? The conversation drifted to the subject of identical twins. "You know," he spoke lowly, "identical twins come from one egg. At the moment of conception there's just one soul, but then the egg divides and becomes two human beings. I believe the soul divides also, each part going into each body. If one of those identical bodies dies at birth, I believe the soul of the dying twin goes into the living twin's body." There was a long pause. "The living twin will have twice the talent, twice the fame—yet also twice the sorrow, twice the pain."

A strange feeling came over me. There was so much thought in what he said. Why was he telling me? Which Orion was calling? If this was the Jimmy Ellis/Orion, why would he feel so deeply about the subject of twins? I asked the question I feared most: "Are you Elvis Presley?"

Another long pause. "No," he said firmly. "Elvis is gone. This is Orion."

Again, I reported this conversation to Carole. Later, at another Orion concert, I talked to the Jimmy Ellis/Orion. His reply did not clear up my dilemma. He did not recall talking to Chris over the telephone, did not recall any conversation whatsoever about the soul and identical twins, but said he did raise horses on a farm in Alabama. Obviously if I didn't have so much proof as to the existence of a masked singer named Orion, and witnesses to my conversations with him, this entire matter would sound ludicrous.

Never once did either Orion *ever* say he was Elvis Presley, but in fact said just the opposite.

Carole and I continued our conversations about Orion-the-singer, SUN RECORD'S role, as well as mounting evidence that pointed to a major cover-up in the death of Elvis Presley.

We also questioned whether Elvis did in fact die?

It's difficult not to vacillate as to what was happening between the years 1978 and 1981: the rush of attention by William Morris, Roz Targ, the publishers and David Dortort gave me confirmation that ORION was special. This together with the sudden appearance of a masked singer, the late night telephone calls, the two Orions, the SUN RECORDS connection, Mae Axton, Bob Neal, 20/20's independent investigation of a cover-up, the misspelled name on the grave, the contradictions in the Medical Examiner's report, constantly made me wonder if indeed unwittingly I had "tuned" into something that written as fiction was instead fact?

I was not the only one asking if Elvis hoaxed his death. In the 1979 June issue of PEOPLE MAGAZINE, Merle Haggard was quoted as saying Elvis Presley's death may have been faked. "It would be the first chance for freedom in his entire life, and it could have been a scheme Colonel Parker dreamed up."

DID ELVIS STAGE HIS OWN DEATH?

PHOTOSCREEN'S January, 1980 issue featured the head-lined story: DID ELVIS STAGE HIS OWN DEATH? " 'It is very possible that Elvis Presley is indeed alive,' " they quote a prominent psychiatrist as telling them. "We felt as if we had been struck by a lightning bolt. When we had approached this doctor to find out if we were on the path of the biggest story of the century or just completely out of our mind, we were leaning to the latter."

Listed are some of the facts presented by the doctor to support the theory that Elvis had hoaxed his death:

Why had Vernon refused to respond to Memphis city officials' request to buy Elvis' estate and preserve it as a park forevermore, despite the fact Vernon said he was anxious to have Elvis' memory enshrined in his adopted hometown?

Why had Elvis' suite in the mansion been preserved intact since his alleged death? "No one is allowed up there even to clean,'' one former Presley pal has told reporters. PHOTOSCREEN questions why the suite was off limits under Vernon Presley's orders. What were they trying to hide?

Imagine my surprise when this article began talking about a mystery singer by the name of Orion Eckley Darnell—the full name of a fictional character I had created! Wasn't this ever going to end?

The PHOTOSCREEN continues by saying, ''. . . we've been told that Elvis imported a lookalike who was very ill and this is the Elvis Presley who was actually buried.''

I had heard another version of this same story: a man from England who looked like Presley, but who was not a singer was terminally ill with cancer. He contacted Elvis and told him about his illness, how poor he was, and that he had no family. He was brought to Graceland and sequestered upstairs where his last days were lived in comfort. He received medical attention.

''That's why I believe those rumors about Elvis having cancer have a basis,'' one fan said. ''It was the other man who had the cancer; the drugs were prescribed for him, not Elvis.''

I suppose anything is possible but I find it hard to accept these theories. Still, the fact is that questions are asked and rumors abound. Where there's smoke, is there fire?

''It's really not as peculiar as you think,'' the doctor continued in regards to Elvis going into hiding. ''You don't realize how many people disappear without a trace every day. Not from foul play, either, but just because they have planned to escape their past. Sometimes it is a bad marriage or just a series of problems that overwhelm them emotionally to the point that they just have to leave. More than we care to talk about have never been found. Elvis may not have been so heartless; he apparently did tell his loved ones where he could be found. Otherwise, no one would be whispering about his staging his own death.''

The whispers have obviously grown louder.

A disc jockey who was with KEEN RADIO in San Jose, California received a strange telephone call in 1981 from a man identifying himself as ''Sivle.'' (That is Elvis spelled backwards.) From what I gather from a copy of that interview, Jay Albright had reason to believe the caller could be Elvis Presley. I have a tape of that interview and I wonder about the voice? It's also worth mentioning that in the book ELVIS IN PRIVATE by Peter Haining there is an interview with Chet Atkins, one of the most accomplished guitarists in the country. He says that Elvis used to book the recording studio under the name "Sivle." There is also on display in an Elvis Presley museum in Florida a bracelet of Elvis' with the name "Sivle." The ELVIS IN PRIVATE book was not released until 1987 thus an imitator might not have known that Elvis used the backward spelling of his name, yet the caller to Mr. Albright knew it six years *prior* to it becoming public knowledge.

One would expect this type of headlined story in the rag magazines and indeed there were many. However, the truth is that the legitimate media was also asking questions. (One magazine actually ran a 1979 Social Strivers Sweepstakes. They listed items like Oddest Couple going to John Travolta and Lily Tomlin, Couples We're Tired Of going to Steve Martin and Bernadette Peters, Burt Reynolds and Hal Needham. **Best Faked Death, Elvis Presley**.)

During this time I visited with Mae Axton at her house in Hendersonville and at other Nashville locations, where we (Carole and Walt Halupke were with me and witnesses to these conversations) met many songwriters who both wrote and worked for Elvis, including Jerry Chestnut, who wrote T-R-O-U-B-L-E and IT'S MIDNIGHT, Ray Pennington who wrote RAMBLIN' MAN, Tex Davis who wrote BE BOB A LULU and John Fisher, of Fish Mann Productions.

Ray said to me, "I think you're right. I think Elvis is alive. Nothing adds up." Ray also spoke of hearing something odd concerning the attitude of Felton Jarvis, Elvis' RCA record promoter. "Felton loved Elvis and Elvis was good to Felton. The day after Elvis' death, Felton was as happy as a lark, whistling, like nothing was wrong. That doesn't make sense . . ."

Another songwriter admitted to us that he went to the private viewing in Memphis. "It wasn't Elvis I can tell you. It looked like a wax dummy. The nose was all wrong. Everything was. I got up close and I can tell you it wasn't

Elvis. I went over to Vernon and asked him what was going on? "That ain't Elvis. . . ."

Vernon nodded and admitted it wasn't.

"Then where is he?"

"Upstairs," Vernon said. "We had to show the fans something."

Another gentleman said he actually ran into Elvis in Atlanta. "I can't believe what I'm seeing?" he said he told Elvis. "I don't believe it!"

He said Elvis adjusted his sunglasses and smiled sheepishly, then said, "Man, you ain't seen me, O.K.?"

To the Elvis TCB Fan Club in Chicago around 1981 or 1982, a telephone call was received from a man who sounded like Elvis Presley. He thanked everyone, and then repeated familiar lyrics which ended with, "this too shall pass away."

Just as one cannot see a face on album recordings, one cannot see a face over the telephone. All of these sightings, all of these telephone calls to the fans, to D.J.'s, to columnists, to me—all could indeed be an elaborate "put on." Much of this could be dismissed if not for other facts. We must also remember that the fans meant a lot to Elvis. In an interview Elvis did in 1962 on a movie set, he stresses the importance of fans. It would not be out of line for him to continue to call them—or notify them of his presence. They, for the most part, do not believe Elvis died, a belief continually reflected in their newsletters. From THE ELVIS SPECIAL:

> "We have received startling news from four different people from Louisville, Kentucky. A TV news program ran a story that a plane has been found registered to Elvis and apparently being lived in by an unknown person. The plane is large, with all the comforts of home and even has a swimming pool area. People are asking if Elvis is living in it."

Under their section "ELVIS' DEATH—COMMENTS AND QUESTIONS:"

> " 'I want to tell you something about the name Sivle. We went to the EP Museum down here in Orlando, Fla. and I saw a name band in the display case that was on Elvis'

wrist—the name was Sivle. I was shocked!'—K. Ferguson, The Presleyites."

Many have said the body brought into Baptist Memorial Hospital was not Elvis.

His contract with Colonel Parker was about to expire. Coincidence?

" 'This may sound like an off-the-wall statement, but if Elvis could pull it off, if he did it, I think the one person who knew about it—and maybe masterminded the whole thing was Colonel Tom Parker.'—C. Ross, Elvis Memorial, Hawaii."

THE ELVIS SPECIAL comments as to why Elvis would go to so much trouble to hoax his death when he could have simply retired?

"Do you really think the fans would have left Elvis alone if he had retired? Even if he stated ill health as the reason? They never left him alone when he was in the hospital, or had to cancel a Vegas/Tahoe stint due to ill health. The fans followed Elvis everywhere regardless of Elvis' feelings. . . . We know of several instances where Elvis fooled his 'best friends' and the fans by disguising himself and even, on occasion, having a double. . . ."

I found their next comment a shocker. It is in regards to a statement made by Dee Presley, the former stepmother of Elvis. "In 1978 Dee Presley told us that she thinks Elvis called her on the telephone. He didn't identify himself but he knew things only Elvis would know!"

More questions from THE ELVIS SPECIAL:

Elvis visited the dentist on the 16th—why weren't there traces of novacaine in his system?

If Elvis' heart was so enlarged how was it possible that he could play racquetball for hours on the 16th?

93

Why is it that Elvis had so little money in a savings account and over a million in a checking account? Easy access? And where is the rest of his money?

Elvis had more property and assets than were listed by the inventory. What happened to them? Were they sold prior to August 16th? By whom?

Why were we (The Elvis Special) personally asked by Vernon Presley NOT to come to Memphis for the funeral but to come a week later?*

Why was the date on Elvis' will crossed off and changed by hand?

Elvis' coffin weighed over 900 pounds. After talking to a mortician, a combining Elvis' weight with the type of coffin there are more than 300 pounds unaccounted for. So what was in there?**

An inventory of Elvis' estate, Graceland, was done by the court shortly after Elvis' death. It lists less than a half dozen pieces of jewelry, no photos, fake suede and leather furniture and clothing and mismatched crystal, silverware, etc. What happened to all of Elvis' jewelry and clothing? Where are all his favorites?

According to Maria Columbus and Jeannie Tessum, co-presidents of THE ELVIS SPECIAL, not only do many fans believe Elvis could be alive, but similar questions arise from those in Elvis' circle. "We ran into Jerry Schilling (a close friend of Elvis) at a local airport restaurant around 1983. He was having lunch with Al Jardine of the Beach Boys and

*In a conversation with Maria she now believes Vernon did not want such loyal fans at the viewing as they would have known it was not Elvis in the coffin. Vernon had not counted on anyone getting a picture. When they saw the picture they knew it wasn't Elvis. The pug nose, the hairline, the brows, the chin—all different.

**Since the fans now say it was a wax dummy in the coffin they believe the weight difference of the coffin is because it contained an air conditioning unit to keep the wax from melting.

admitted that rumors were running rampant among Elvis' group that he isn't dead and he asked us to confirm! We just laughed and said, 'thought you were all such good friends.'"

The ROUSTABOUT fan newsletter states that "a Pennsylvania fan talking to Charlie Hodge (a close friend of Elvis') was told, 'Elvis hasn't left us, he's just changed his address.' An odd choice of words, huh?"

ROUSTABOUT received a letter from someone who asked to remain anonymous because he would lose his job if his identity was known. The letter states that this person had a friend who worked at the reservations desk at the Memphis airport. "She didn't think too much of it at the time. She remembers that on August 17th, a man bearing a slight resemblance to Elvis picked up a ticket to Buenos Aires which had been reserved under the name of John Burrows. Knowing the death of Elvis the day before, she, of course, did not really think it was him. But she told me later that although he wore dark glasses and wore rather plain looking clothing, Elvis was the first person she thought of as 'John Burrows' paid for that ticket."

John Burrows (Remember that a ticket to South America was bought the day after Elvis's death, by a man called John Burrows, who resembled greatly, Elvis Presley), was the code name Elvis Presley used—it was the name he gave to personal friends, including President Richard Nixon, if they needed to get through to him. The speculation as to why Elvis would fly commercial rather than use one of his private planes is because it would be noticed landing anywhere it went. And secondly, with all the Elvis lookalikes in Memphis at the time of his "death," he would not stand out at the airport. ROUSTABOUT further speculates that since Elvis used that code name when he was appointed a special agent of the Bureau of Narcotics and Dangerous Drugs, he may have been issued such items as a passport or a birth certificate in that name.

Some historians say Elvis used the Burroughs spelling as well. Historically there is another John Burroughs, a philosopher and thinker. Elvis was a student of these subjects and may have used this name for personal reasons.

ROUSTABOUT quotes Charlie Hodge as mentioning, "he might be moving to Costa Rica . . . an odd place to live, huh?"

ROUSTABOUT also raised this point: "I wouldn't want to suggest Elvis was getting rid of things he'd no longer need, but he sold the ranch on August 10th."

And this: "Want to play Sherlock? What will you obviously deduct from the following press clipping: 'A $23,789.73 claim—filed against the estate of Elvis Presley for the entertainer's funeral expenses has been settled, officials said today. Officials said that the moving of Gladys Presley, the singer's mother, were settled Thursday.' They just dropped an Atomic Bomb but nobody caught on. Read that again. It's clear as a bell. The charges were for moving the body of Elvis' mother. Not Elvis. Vernon received no such bill for his body. Did they move him for free out of the kindness of their hearts. Draw your own deductions . . ."

Whether the fans via their newsletters have their facts 100% correct is questionable. No one, not even the major media sources, has been able to get correct information. What is interesting is that the fans' questions arise from the belief that Elvis is *not* dead. They also question as to why authorized Elvis merchandise was available for fans at Memphis on August 17, 1977? "It was there in large quantities a lot sooner than it had a right to be," they claim. In Indianapolis, the RCA Victor pressing plant was inundated with orders. It began to press Elvis' records at a rate of 250,000 albums or 200,000 singles a day. The expected demand was 100 million, based on the fact that 20 million were sold the day following Elvis' death. What these figures also mean is that 20 million discs were already in the stores waiting to be sold. Is it coincidence that on June 25th and June 26th Elvis performed in Indianapolis? This was approximately six weeks before his "death."

Many believe that the August 16, 1977 scheduled tour was for two reasons: one, as an excuse to have merchandise ready for sale, and secondly, to have as many people as possible away from the mansion. Still, since only 12 shows were scheduled, 20 million discs is an incredible number. Whatever the numbers, whatever deductions one makes, the Elvis merchandising machine was in mind-boggling motion.

Also asked is this question: why would Elvis, so overweight and looking terrible, allow for a million dollar television special during his last tour? The fans analyzed it was because "he needed all the money possible and quickly." They also ask how a "specially designed 900 pound coffin was flown into Memphis on such short notice?"

Many of the fans tore to pieces the coffin photo which appeared in THE NATIONAL ENQUIRER stating, "Elvis has a forehead, nose and chin that he never had before." They also found suspicious the singular "episode of Elvis leaving us the same week as his mother, the odds against that 52 to 1."

Besides questioning "cause of death," they wonder why Vernon, after having sold the Lisa Marie continued to keep "two of Elvis' planes, which are still making unscheduled, unannounced flights?"

And, "why did Elvis change his will only months before disinheriting all his longtime friends and leaving everything to Lisa and Vernon knowing he would be outliving Vernon by decades?" Also questioned were trips made by Vernon to the Dominican Republic? (This falls in line with the John Burrows/South American story.)

Questioned also are anonymous donations in huge amounts to charities Elvis supported during his life. The fans' questions go on and on. "Why was he laid out in a cheap white suit rather than a familiar jumpsuit?"

"If the body was so heavy that it took five people to lift it, how was it possible for Ginger to turn the body over easily?"

"Why the consistent, 'I did not recognize him,' or 'It did not look like him' by technicians, nurses, guards, doctors?"

"Why did one Memphis attorney state in regards to the two men arrested for the body-napping episode, 'If they ever open up this can of worms, I'm afraid somebody is going to be embarrassed,' while another writer stated publically that 'the death of Elvis Presley was a story not over—that it could erupt into a national sensation at any time'?"

The fans have a right to their questions. They loved and still love Elvis Presley. They know more about his habits, his tastes, and his thoughts, than they probably know about their closest friends. Their questions are worthy of recognition. The fans of Elvis Presley are probably the largest captured market in the world. They are his golden hen. That so many of them believe Elvis Presley never died on August 16, 1977 is highly significant and could warrant a treatise in itself. At first I thought this was a case of not wanting to believe their king was dead. Now I realize, because of what happened to me and my novel ORION together with independent media investigation, that their questions have validity.

Because ORION became scarce, the novel has become a collector's item. The August 17, 1987 issue of PEOPLE MAGAZINE featured a front page story on ELVIS, Ten years Later. The inside related story pictured a woman who started a collection of Elvisbilia. ORION was also pictured as a collector's item.

I've had terrific input from Elvis fans such as Maria Columbus and Marilou Schuster. When I think I want to get on with other projects they telephone and urge that I continue. They know my material is documented.

They ask continually about what happened to the novel ORION.

They believe Elvis Presley is alive.

They believe that the disappearance of a fictional book that shows how a death is hoaxed and the death of Elvis Presley is connected. They want to know the truth.

So do I.

FORMERLY FRANZ J.
OBEN ASSOCIATES, INC.

CABLE ADDRESS
ROSBOOKS NEW YORK
TELEX 63 100

Roslyn Targ

LITERARY AGENCY, INC.

250 WEST 57TH STREET, NEW YORK, N. Y. 10019 · TELEPHONE (212) 582-4210

February 25, 1980

Dearest Gail:

What a lovely surprise to receive your glorious plant on Saturday.
It has been such a hectic week for me that I just didn't get a
chance to call you, and I was suffering from exhaustion all week-
end. We are on our way. I'm really very happy. The market at
the moment is horrible, therefore I'm truly pleased to have gotten
the $60,000 from Pocket Books. The publisher of Pocket Books was
at Ballantines and published an Elvis Presley book which sold,
5,000,000 copies. I know that he is very high on ORION. *this book soon.*

Yours,

RT/na

MEMBER SOCIETY OF AUTHORS' REPRESENTATIVES

RoslynTarg
LITERARY AGENCY, INC.
250 WEST 57TH STREET, NEW YORK, N.Y. 10019
TELEPHONE (212) 682-4210

3/11/80

Dear Carol:

I've been meaning to write to you for
some time now, but my office is so
hectic that the letter seems to be
postponed each day.

I can't tell you how grateful I am
that you recommended Gail Brewer-
Giorgio to me. I think she has an
exciting talent, and I'm so happy
that I was able to place ORION with
Pocket Books. I look forward to
placing motion picture rights and
foreign rights.

I do hope one day I shall have the
opportunity to meet you and thank you
personally.

In the meantime may I send you...

My warmest regards,
(Bill joins me in doing so)

Roslyn Targ

RT/na

FORMERLY FRANZ J
HORCH ASSOCIATES, INC.

CABLE ADDRESS
ROSBOOKS NEW YORK
TELEX 62 193

Roslyn Targ
LITERARY AGENCY, INC.

250 WEST 57TH STREET, NEW YORK, N.Y. 10107

TELEPHONE (212) 582-4210

April 28, 1982

Dear Gail:

I've just received copies of the Dutch
edition of ORION (DE KONING VAN DE
ROCK'N ROLL). I noticed that a trade
publisher's name, Elsevier, was mentioned.
I have written to ECI pointing out that
we are supposed to receive ninety percent
of the proceeds of any sale to a trade
house and also to receive copy of the
contract. The moment I have more information I shall be in touch, but in the
meantime I'm sending you copies of the
edition.

Yours,

RT/na
cc: Norman Shavin

MEMBER SOCIETY OF AUTHORS' REPRESENTATIVES

THE DESECRATION

As you peruse personal correspondence, especially those letters from my former New York literary agent Roslyn Targ and Simon and Schuster's Pocket Books division, you'll note that ORION received a large advance. The Holland hardback rights were also sold. Movie interest was accelerating. Naturally I had good reason to be in top spirits. I continued to state to the press that ORION was fiction and that despite the media's independent investigation about something being terribly wrong in the Elvis Presley camp, I endeavored to maintain my book's own literary identity: ORION was fictional. I stressed I had never known Elvis Presley, never had met his family, never had been to Memphis. I further stressed that ORION had been created *prior* to the media's investigation and that, yes, I was as amazed as anyone that so much of what I had created via fiction was becoming fact.

There were the obvious questions and confusion concerning the singer Orion as well as the possibility of two masked men. There were the telephone calls from a mysterious voice. There were the endless calls from fans who believed Elvis did not die and who wanted to know if I knew something. I told them I had no real information concerning Elvis Presley and a cover-up and in fact was not collecting data but was instead concentrating on the novel's release.

ORION was slated to be published August 1981. I was in communication with the publisher in New York and because of their enthusiasm, the $60,000 advance, letters and verbal promises, I was confident that a vigorous publicity campaign would be mounted. After all, radio and television stations across the country, as well as the print media, were already focusing in on ORION and without publicity and full support of the publisher most books face an almost certain death. My first clue that a problem existed came in the following letter:

Pocket Books

May 14, 1981

Dear Gail:

Now that we're in the middle of May, it's time to start making plans
for ABA and for the publicity of ORION. I hope we'll be able to
meet at ABA, but more about that later.

First, I'd like to explain the publicity situation with ORION. I
recently had a meeting with the Pocket Books attorney about our
publicity plans for ORION. In order to avoid any possible litigation
on this book, she has advised us against making any connection between Orion and Elvis Presley on the cover, the press release, or
any material coming out of Pocket Books, both written and verbal.
As a result of these restrictions, it seems unlikely that we will
be able to project ORION to the media in a way that will meet your
expectations. What this means is that we will be unable to set up
interviews for you.

Gail, there are, however, many outlets left open to us. We will be
sending out our Pocket Preview, featuring ORION, to over 7,500
reviewers. A copy of this is enclosed. We will also send review
copies with a press release to media people all over the U.S. as
well as our Country & Western lists plus any others you supply.
However, as mentioned, on neither our cover copy, our press materials,
nor in discussions with the media, can there be any mention of Elvis
Presley. Nor can this subject be discussed in setting up television,
magazine, or newspaper interviews.

I understand that you have some very good connections with <u>People</u> and
<u>Us</u> magazines and I do encourage you to pursue your plans for ORION.
We do, however, strongly advise that you follow these guidelines
set by our attorney.

I do hope we can meet at ABA. How about Sunday? Let me know if you
can come to our booth and meet Pocket Books people and have lunch.
Please call me or Anne Maitland, Associate Publicity Director, at
the Hyatt Regency in Atlanta or I'll try to reach you and we can
arrange to get you a guest pass. Also, I'll be at Pocket Books
until May 21. I depart for Atlanta on the 22nd.

Best,

Carol Fass

Simon & Schuster Building
1230 Avenue of the Americas
New York, NY 10020
212 246 2121

I couldn't understand why they were so afraid of litigation? The novel had been purchased quite a while ago; they knew the novel was born of fiction. They even knew that the book had been copyrighted prior to fiction perhaps becoming fact. How could I be penalized for writing about things I knew nothing about and which had only come to light years after I created ORION? If there was an artistic connection to Elvis, so what? Everything created artistically is inspired by something or someone. Plus there was nothing via fiction that would defame Elvis Presley or anyone close to him. The opposite was true. I could prove quite easily, if asked, that ORION was created from a composite of religion, mythology, philosophy and a contemporary hero.

Being told that I could never mention Elvis Presley in connection with ORION was confusing. Those questions were already being asked since the mysterious singer Orion arrived on the scene. The publishers knew about 20/20's show on the cover-up in the death of Elvis Presley. 20/20's show had been aired before they even purchased ORION. Questions were already being asked. How could I avoid being asked about Elvis in connection with ORION? And if I were asked about Elvis and ORION? I would tell the media the truth: ORION was fictional.

I felt muzzled. But I didn't know why.

My publisher did not want me to discuss Elvis Presley in connection with ORION. Yet was it coincidence that they chose August for the novel's release knowing full well that August was the anniversary of the death of Elvis Presley? Was it coincidence that on their own promotional material sent out they used the following quote:

"ORION is the kind of book that intrigues the reader, challenges the 'factual' and stirs the heart. It melds the humor, the pathos . . . the ecstasy and the tragedy, and leaves you wondering."

—Mae Boren Axton, co-author of the song, "Heartbreak Hotel"

I reread the promotion, reread the part where Mae Axton stated ORION challenged the 'factual' and I wondered. Mae had been very close to Elvis. Her choice of words was

FOR IMMEDIATE RELEASE
CONTACT: Linda Vilensky

NEWS FROM

POCKET BOOKS

CAROL FASS, DIRECTOR OF PUBLICITY   1230 AVENUE OF THE AMERICAS   NEW YORK, NEW YORK 10020 (212)246-2121

ORION: The Living Superstar of Song

Pocket Books Publishes the Amazing Novel That Launched
the Career of a New Country-Western Singing Star

> "ORION is the kind of book that intrigues the reader,
> challenges the 'factual' and stirs the heart. It melds
> the humor, the pathos...the ecstasy and the tragedy, and
> leaves you wondering."
>
> -- Mae Boren Axton, co-author of
>   the song, "Heartbreak Hotel"

There are many instances where truth is stranger than fiction. In the case of ORION: The Living Superstar of Song (August 1981/$3.50), the fictional story and the real story behind it are equally incredible. Gail Brewer-Giorgio's novel about a rock-and-roll superstar who stages his own death to escape the rigors of fame has been responsible for launching the career of an up-and-coming singing star named Orion.

The novel chronicles the rise of Orion Eckley Darnell, a poor Southern boy who dreamed of making a career out of singing and bringing his own special brand of music to the world. After surviving hundreds of frustrations and dead ends, he made his break-through to fame. But he wasn't prepared for the greatest trial of all: the heartbreaking loneliness that only a man loved by millions could feel. For Orion, there was only one way out...

Orion's moving story has been the impetus for a real-life Orion who is creating a sensation in country-western circles. After Ms. Brewer-Giorgio wrote ORION, she received a phone call from a man who said, "Orion is born today." Many people are now watching the career of this new star, born out of

MORE...

interesting but rather than explore it at that moment, I was more interested in finding out why the very publisher who asked me not to mention Elvis Presley in connection with ORION had not only chosen Elvis' August death anniversary to release ORION, but had used the quote of the one person who would be most connected with Elvis—the woman who co-wrote Elvis's first million seller, HEARTBREAK HOTEL.

The novel was released toward the end of August. As summer went into fall, there were book signings. The media was zooming in and the project was gaining momentum. September was entering October, then November. By January, the book was gone. It was off the shelves. I was receiving telephone calls from across the nation asking how to get the novel ORION? People had gone into bookstores asking to buy the novel. It was gone. It was not orderable.

"It's out of print," the stores and their customers were told.

This made no sense. Even without publicity the novel had sold close to 70,000 copies in a short period of time. (This number does not reflect the hardback, collector's editions or Holland editions.) I telephoned the publisher, left my name but never received call backs. My attorney wrote. No response. In the meantime I kept getting calls from people wanting the novel. Frustration was changing to curiosity to anger. Finally I contacted one of the distributors. He didn't know the real story and said, "I thought ORION was doing well. I don't know . . . I was told to pull the book."

I asked him if he could find out why since no matter when my attorney or I called we were never called back. He said he would try to do his best. Eventually he got back to me saying that he was told the book was pulled because it was not doing that well.

Perhaps 70,000 copies in a few months is not a good sale, but without publicity it seemed so. The novel wasn't out long enough to measure the good or bad results. I contacted my agent but her original enthusiasm in ORION had suddenly disappeared. She still loved the book but seemed tired of the ORION project and had other books to sell. I did not want my frustration to sound like sour grapes or to sever our position as friends. She and her husband Bill meant too much to me to cry "foul play." I even suspect she tried to find out

Pocket Books

Martin Asher
Editor-in-Chief

May 19, 1981

Dear Gail:

Thank you for your letter of May 1 and all the praise for the ORION cover. I've passed your compliments along to the appropriate people. It is indeed nice to know when one's efforts are appreciated.

I've been forwarding the publicity material to Carol Fass, our publicity director. You have been so diligent in getting it to us, and I know Carol appreciates your help. I apologize for not acknowledging all your notes sooner, but we have been very busy planning for ABA and attending regional sales conferences. Pocket Books does indeed have "real people" who are looking forward to the publication and success of ORION.

Sincerely,

Marty Asher

MA/tt

Simon & Schuster Building
1230 Avenue of the Americas
New York, NY 10020
212 246 2121

Pocket Books

July 9, 1981

Dear Gail:

It was wonderful speaking with you last week. I hope that sometime soon we can meet!

I have enclosed some material which I think will help you in the ORION publicity campaign. Included are 100 press releases and the names and addresses of national T.V. contacts. I've also ordered 100 books which will be sent to you directly from our warehouse.

Regarding your question of the correct spelling of some Pocket Books people's names - they are spelled - George Schneider and Robin Warner.

I hope that all of this will be of help to you. If I can do anything else for you, please feel free to call.

Best,

Linda

Linda Vilensky
Publicist
212/246-2121, x253,254

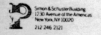
Simon & Schuster Building
1230 Avenue of the Americas
New York, NY 10020
212 246 2121

what was happening, but she had only so much time to spare on one writer. Also she had to work with Simon and Schuster and Pocket Books on other projects, and it would not be professionally good for me to ruffle feathers. I must also say that Roz, like myself, really had no understanding of the bigger picture. Had she known what I now know I am sure she would have rallied to my defense. She is the model of integrity. At that time, though, we had no reason to believe there was something to defend. (Roz also did not know about my history with William Morris as it did not seem relevant at the time.)

I was allowed to keep the large advance. But I was also paralyzed. Where I once feared a three year exclusive with William Morris would keep my manuscript on their shelves, I now found my contract with a publisher kept ORION off the bookshelves!

How many Goliaths were there?

What could I do? I no longer owned the rights to ORION. I could not sell them to any U.S. publisher. Yet while I was crying over what happened to ORION, I had the feeling that somewhere, someplace, someone was smiling.

Poor David. Goliath was indeed an enormous Giant!

Having not yet heard that ORION had disappeared, the movie interest continued. I did not want to jeopardize movie interest and prayed for "something to happen to set things right." I knew it would be only a matter of time before it became apparent to the movie people that ORION was no more. In the meantime another book was climbing the bestseller list, ELVIS by Albert Goldman—a work that in no way made Elvis out to be a special human being. Albert Goldman was highly critical of Elvis and of the Colonel. The fans in general said they did not like the book.

Yet ORION—which was fiction and which complimented a man like Elvis—became a target of fear. Why?

I purchased ELVIS and was astounded to discover how closely ORION resembled Elvis. Goldman's ELVIS had only recently been released thus ORION could not have used Goldman as a basis of research. I was further amazed when I discovered the Elvis/Jesus connection, a connection I had no way of knowing but wrote via fiction in ORION. Then I began Chapter ten of ELVIS. My hands began to shake. It

111

concerned the close relationship between Colonel Tom Parker and the William Morris Agency. The William Morris Agency represented "Elvis throughout his entire career, and its president, Abe Lastfogel, is one of the Colonel's closest associates . . ."

William Morris. Elvis Presley. Colonel Tom Parker. Bob Neal. Abe Lastfogel.

Until that reading, I had *never* known that the William Morris Agency represented Elvis Presley and Colonel Tom Parker! Neither Bob Neal nor anyone in the Morris Agency ever told me this! The very people who had courted me were the Colonel's best buddies and business associates! (William Morris later represented Priscilla Presley in her best-seller ELVIS AND ME.)

Throughout Mr. Goldman's book is the mention of some of the people who were in contact with me—advising me to give them an exclusive on the handling of ORION, suggesting I not show the manuscript to anyone. I reread their letters, noted how anxious they were, noted also that it was the "ending of ORION" which was fascinating—an ending whereby a singer *and* his famous manager hoax a death!

Was it possible that in this day and age censorship had occurred? Or was it possible my novel had touched upon something? Had ORION become the victim of a cover-up because it exposed a cover-up? How could I possibly find out? Who would talk to me? I called William Morris. No one called back. I tried contacting the New York office, the Nashville office, the west coast office. Nothing. Could it be possible that the people closest to the Colonel were courting me *only* to stop me?

Who would admit such a thing?

Everyone agreed that the William Morris Agency is a giant in the literary world. It would be ill-advised for me to make any connections between the demise of ORION, the Colonel, William Morris, or the publisher. "There is no way you can win even if you proved a connection. No publisher, no agent, no editor would want to buck William Morris. Professionally— whether you suspect and can document the possibility you were a victim—you'll end up being hurt."

I continued to see-saw with both my questions and answers. The William Morris Agency had been very polite. I

112

could not accuse anyone of anything. Although it seemed unlikely, everything that had happened with the ORION project must be chalked up to coincidence. Yet I couldn't help replay the conversations and meetings with representatives from William Morris. Why had I been so hesitant to sign with them? Were my instincts to be trusted?

Secretly I cried into my pillow. True, keeping the money was fine. Yet I felt like I had given birth to a beautiful baby and then after its birth having it aborted!

Through writer Maxine Rock I contacted her New York agent. She in turn called my former editor who had since left the publishing house and was with a national syndicate.

"Hearing the name ORION is a ghost from the past," the editor told the agent. She said it was rumored that the Colonel went to the head of Simon and Schuster, something was worked out, and the book was "hung."

The agent wrote me about this matter. I have purposely deleted her name from the letter because, one, she did me a favor. And, two, she must deal on a daily basis with the top publishers and editors, Simon and Schuster included. I would not want to do anything to jeopardize her position in the literary pecking order. "Most of the major publishers depend on William Morris for some top writers," one editor told me. "It's certainly not a good financial move for a publisher to cross them."

"If the Colonel had someone at William Morris go to Simon and Schuster with the request that ORION be stopped, perhaps with the threat of possible litigation, then the publisher might acquiese?" I asked.

"William Morris is powerful. You're a virgin writer, expendable. For instance if a powerful agent with some top writers goes to a certain house he has bargaining power. He can use his stable of money-makers to an advantage. Multiply that theory a thousand times over with William Morris and you have your answer."

It was obvious there was little I could do. I could prove my connection with the William Morris Agency. I could prove the Colonel and Elvis' connection with the William Morris Agency. I could prove a connection between the William Morris Agency and Simon and Schuster. I could prove ORION was gone. What I couldn't prove, was did it all connect?

October 3, 1983

Dear Gail:

I am most impressed with ORION and, after doing as much detective work as I could without compromising either of us, I mourn its fate at the hands of timid publishers. Indeed, ORION was "hung out to dry." Both the lawyer at S&S at the time and the editors still there admit that they were all afraid of the Colonel and legal problems and simply wrote the book off.

As things haven't changed in that regard I'm afraid other publishers would have the same feelings today so I don't think there is much of a chance of resurrecting ORION (excuse the pun) through normal publishing channels as the Presley estate is still most aggressive in protecting his name (this is true, too, of Marilyn Monroe).

A book-about-the-book could bring some adventurous publisher out of the wood work - or, barring that - perhaps enable you to publish it yourself once the rights are returned. I feel sure a writer capable of producing ORION has many more ideas for future books and the skill to carry them out. Why don't we move forward on that front and handle ORION's future down the line a bit when we get the opportunity to exploit it through other means.

You sound incredibly busy but when you have a moment I'd like to see the outline for the sequel.

Best regards,

Film America

Corporate Office
3132 Randolph Rd., N.E.
Atlanta, Ga. 30345
404-261-3735

Production Office
404-261-3718

GAIL —

WHAT A FABULOUS MEETING!
CAN'T WAIT TO TRY THE
WATERS AND BRING
ORION TO THE SCREEN!

THE ENCLOSED LETTER IS
FOR MR. SNIPES (+ copy for you)

THE BOOK "SCREENPLAY" IS A
VERY GOOD REFERENCE
AND SHOULD BE OF HELP.

BEST WISHES,

25 Jan. 52

Mr. Norman Shavin

President
Capricorn Corporation
4961 Rebel Trail, NW
Atlanta, Georgia 30327

        and

Mr. Avrum Fine

President
FilmAmerica
3132 Randolph Road, NE
Atlanta, Georgia 30345

Dear Norm and Avrum:

    It was a great pleasure meeting with you both recently in Atlanta to explore
the possibilities of converting the book "Orion" into a movie. As you know, I came
to Atlanta specifically for this purpose, and our candid sessions were both
rewarding and most encouraging toward our mutual goal.

    I was impressed by the fact that Capricorn Corp., as publishers, issued the
hardcover edition of this work of fiction by Marietta author Gail Brewer-Giorgio,
and by Capricorn's very prompt sale of the paperback rights to Pocket Books, a
division of Simon & Schuster, as well as to a Dutch publisher for a foreign-
language version.

    I have known Gail for two years and am no stranger to her unusual book. I
believe very strongly that "Orion," which I foresee being converted to a film
to be made in Georgia, can be enormously successful in theatres as well as on TV.

    As you know, I have worked in film, primarily for TV, as both writer and
producer for 30 years. As the current President of the Producers Guild of America,
Inc., I believe I have a keen grasp of the artistic and financial aspects of
film-making, as well as the marketing capability.

    I am eager to accept the role you both suggested, as producer of the movie,
with FilmAmerica as the production company, assuming we can arrange mutually
satisfactory financial and contractual agreements among us.

    You will need to generate some "seed money" from investors to allow FilmAmerica
to acquire the screen rights to the book from Capricorn, which has the sole authority
to negotiate all rights, and to fund the development of a screenplay and secure
commitments from a prime director and first-rank talent.

    I can then present to the TV networks and/or cable-TV systems an opportunity
for them to make a pre-production purchase of the final film. If successful (and
this is a common process in funding and developing films), such pre-production sales
could more than offset costs even before the film is begun. Further, I could become
involved in arranging theatrical distribution in domestic and foreign markets, as
well as helping develop ancillary sales programs.

I believe a "P" or "GP"-rated movie of great quality can be made totally in Georgia for approximately $4 million, which is perhaps less than half the cost of developing it in Hollywood. And I believe the finished product could generate as much as $75 million.

"Orion" is the kind of property I have long sought, and here's why.

The mood of the country shows that people are eager for a film with "Orion's" themes: courage, hope, faith, and a return to the basic values of life. Gail has woven all these elements into a touching, engrossing work of warm fiction about a folksinger who rises from poor Southern roots to achieve extraordinary acclaim. How the folksinger "Orion" handles the enormous pressures of fame, how public worship nearly destroys the man and all he loves, and how public adulation changes those who worship him---these are themes both contemporary and ancient.

This can be a most dramatic film, a powerful movie of the kind for which there is a public hunger, without falling into the usual Hollywood inclusion of outrageous violence.

I encourage you to seek the funds necessary to bring this project to the initial stages of fruition. Toward that purpose, I would be delighted to return to Atlanta, at a time convenient to us all, to meet with such investors who would be free, without any prior commitment, to ask any questions and secure first-hand details of my own desire to be involved, and how they can take part.

While there are few guarantees in this world, there are opportunities which, when carefully nurtured, have the seeds of maturing into excellent properties which may generate unusual rewards.

I believe "Orion" represents just such an opportunity.

I look forward to hearing from you.

Best personal regards,

David Dortort

David Dortort

Corporate Office   Production Office
3132 Randolph Rd., N.E. 404 — 261-3718
Atlanta, Ga. 30345
404 — 261-3735

DAVID DORTORT, producer of <u>Bonanza</u>, the longest running and most successful dramatic series in television history, today announced his collaboration with Atlanta businessman and film industry veteran AVRUM FINE to develop and produce motion pictures for filming in Georgia.

Fine, whose FilmAmerica, Inc. will be the production company for the projects, was obviously elated over the association with Dortort. "When you talk about David Dortort, you're talking about a part of Hollywood history", states Fine. "He's been a writer, director and producer for thirty years. He pioneered color programming with the first regularly broadcast series in American television. Of course, in addition to <u>Bonanza</u>, David's series credits include <u>The Chisholms</u> and <u>The High Chaparral</u>. David also holds the distinction of serving as president of both the Writers Guild of America and the equally prestigious Producers Guild of America."

According to Fine, what started the ball rolling was Dortort's desire to bring to the screen the book <u>Orion</u>, written by Atlanta author Gail Brewer-Giorgio. Gail called Avrum in on the project last summer after Dortort contacted her expressing serious interest in the book. Fine recounts several meetings with Dortort in Atlanta on the film project. "One thing led to another", recalls Fine, "and now we're considering a slate of productions that could be filmed entirely in Georgia." "But, our first commitment is to <u>Orion</u>, and to this end David is devoting a lot of time and energy."

Closely allied with the filming of <u>Orion</u> is Norman Shavin, one of Atlanta's best known writers and publishers. Shavin will oversee all negotiations for acquisition of film and ancillary rights to the book and characters through his firm the Capricorn Corporation.

Since its release in 1980, <u>Orion</u> has received quite a bit of press because of its remarkable story of the rural South and one of its sons who rose to become an idol to millions the world over. The striking picture of Americana portrayed in the book is what attracted producer Dortort to the property.

(MORE)

Corporate Office
3132 Randolph Rd., N.E.
Atlanta, Ga. 30345
404-261-3735

Production Office
404-261-3718

According to Fine, financing for the venture is now being worked out. "We're in touch with the investment community here in Atlanta and there has been a great deal of interest shown, indeed," he reports.

Fine is most proud of the potential these plans have for making Atlanta a major film center. "It is exciting to think of what this means to all the film professionals who have stuck it out for so many years here," he states. "And that pleases me most of all."

"BONANZA" PRODUCER TO FILM IN GEORGIA

A WEEK AFTER ANNOUNCING HIS COLLABORATION WITH HOLLYWOOD PRODUCER DAVID DORTORT (BONANZA, THE CHISHOLMS, THE HIGH CHAPARRAL), ATLANTA BUSINESSMAN AVRUM FINE DISCLOSED THAT A SLATE OF SEVEN FILMS IS BEING CONSIDERED FOR PRODUCTION IN GEORGIA BY DORTORT AND FILMAMERICA, INC.

"THIS COULD MEAN A LONG-TERM ASSOCIATION BETWEEN FILMAMERICA AND MR. DORTORT" STATES FINE.

FINE DESCRIBES MOST OF THE PROJECTS AS HAVING A DISTINCTIVE FLAVOR OF AMERICANA. "THAT'S A SUBJECT ABOUT WHICH DAVID DORTORT IS QUITE FAMILIAR" HE CONTINUES. FINE COULD NOT DISCUSS THE SPECIFICS OF THE STORIES BUT DID OFFER A GLIMPSE OF THEIR CONTENT AS "ADVENTURES THAT ARE FILLED WITH THE VERY STUFF THAT MAKES AMERICA SUCH A REMARKABLE LAND."

FINE AND DORTORT FIRST CAME TOGETHER LAST OCTOBER ON A PROJECT OF MUTUTUAL INTEREST: BRINGING TO THE SCREEN THE NOVEL ORION, WRITTEN BY ATLANTA AUTHOR GAIL BREWER-GIORGIO. "THE PAPERBACK VERSION HAS JUST HIT LOCAL SHELVES, AND IS SELLING BRISKLY" ACCORDING TO FINE. THE STORY TRACES THE LIFE OF A YOUNG MAN WHO RISES FROM HIS BACKWOODS BEGINNINGS TO BECOME THE OBJECT OF THE WORLD'S DESIRE AS THE GREATEST SINGER OF HIS TIME, ONLY TO LOSE HIS VERY SOUL TO A DEMANDING PUBLIC. HIS WAY OF GETTING AWAY FROM THE WORLD AND OF REDEEMING HIS IDENTITY HAS BEEN THE SUBJECT OF CONTROVERSY IN THE NATION'S PRESS SINCE THE HARDCOVER'S RELEASE TWO YEARS AGO. . DORTORT HAD BEEN INTERESTED IN THE BOOK FOR SOME TIME AND WAS INTRODUCED TO FINE BY MRS. GIORGIO.

DORTORT IS PERHAPS BEST KNOWN AS THE CREATOR AND PRODUCER OF BONANZA, THE LONGEST-RUNNING DRAMATIC SERIES IN TELEVISION HISTORY AND THE FIRST TO BRING COLOR TO THE AMERICAN VIEWER ON A REGULAR BASIS. THE PRODUCER HAS BEEN PRESIDENT OF THE WRITERS GUILD OF AMERICA AND IS NOW SERVING AS PRESIDENT OF THE PRODUCERS GUILD OF AMERICA.

"HE'S QUITE A PART OF HOLLYWOOD HISTORY" SAYS FINE. "AND I'M JUST DELIGHTED WITH THE PROSPECT OF HAVING HIM PRODUCE IN GEORGIA".

-30-

For More Information, Contact Avrum Fine at (404) 261-3718/261-3735

I doubt very much if the Colonel would physically walk into any New York publisher's office. If such a thing had been done it would seem reasonable that the Colonel would have used his representatives—in this case William Morris. Would William Morris be capable of that sort of thing?

Giving everyone the benefit of doubt, I tried everything possible to sort it all out. I usually ended up full circle in my questioning. In the meantime the mysterious masked singer Orion was also disappearing. I believe in coincidence but all of this was too coincidental. Over and over I studied the floating pieces of the puzzle: a fictional book, agents, publishers, the power of money, a mystery singer (or two of them), movie producers—then nothing.

"I can't understand why the singer has also disappeared," I mentioned to one of my attorneys.

"It could all be connected. Since you managed to get a contract 'in spite of,' maybe the Orion/singer thing was a safeguard."

"I don't understand . . . ?"

"It could have been another way of stopping the book, of making sure no one took it seriously. People would think it was about this Long Ranger singer—that it was hokey, a gimmick."

The entire ORION project was too bizarre to believe. Also too bizarre to believe was that ORION was unintentionally the weed in someone's bed of roses. I was too insignificant in importance to be part of a conspiracy. Wasn't I?

Yet without design or intention I had become the hub of a many-spoked wheel.

People continued to call. Fans sent me information and questions. They wanted to hear what I had to say. Yet what could I say? I never intimated Elvis Presley was alive. I never wanted to play Geraldo Rivera and do an investigative piece on the cover-up in the death of Elvis Presley. All I wanted was to earn a living as a writer of fiction.

I tried to let the ORION matter drop. My family life was suffering. I hurt inside. I decided to go back and work on the novel I had begun prior to writing ORION, now entitled DREAM OF THE VAGABOND. I had the first draft copyrighted in October of 1979. This is important to note because of what has since occurred with that novel—and how it fits into the ORION picture.

DREAM OF THE VAGABOND concerns the downfall of a Presidential political candidate due to his clandestine meetings with a young woman. The press had this candidate followed and as a 'god machine,' they are responsible for his having to pull out of the race, leaving the door open for a popular black candidate.

Remember, this novel was copyrighted eight years *before* the Gary Hart scandal.

In June of 1987 there was a headlined story concerning DREAM OF THE VAGABOND in which I was interviewed. "I was shocked when I read the news concerning Gary Hart and his meetings with Donna Rice. That it was the power of the press which confronted him with evidence strong enough to force him to withdraw from the presidential race was further astounding. And when the political door was opened to Jesse Jackson, a powerful black leader, I was even more shocked. It was exactly like my novel which was first copyrighted in October of 1979," I told the interviewer.

One of my central characters is named Michael Garber. He's followed by the press and is the subject of a stakeout. The story of Michael Garber is amazingly close to that of Gary Hart. Both Garber and Hart are idealists and both get caught with their "pants down."

In DREAM OF THE VAGABOND there is a conspiracy behind the Presidential withdrawal. In the end it is a power play, although the reader is left with the idea that Garber will somehow, someday make his political comeback—which, of course, is what Gary Hart recently did.

There are many other major scenes in DREAM OF THE VAGABOND which came true *after* I wrote about them. One concerns the firebombing of a black neighborhood near Philadelphia—caused by the actions of a black radical group called FIRE. Incredibly, in May of 1985, a black neighborhood in Philadelphia was firebombed. The group that prompted the attack was called MOVE. The MOVE fire and the reasons surrounding it were so close to what I had written as fiction that it was eerie.

This novel is full of events which have come true and some which I think could be true.

One in particular concerns a young lady named Davee O'Hanlon. She's politically outspoken, especially about the war in Vietnam. She's very Jane Fondish. There comes a point where she is actually contacted by our government to go to Hanoi as a secret agent. Our government warns her that if she is caught they will deny all connection with her. They know that since she is so vocally against the war in Vietnam that there is a good chance she will be a welcomed guest in Hanoi, although in America she will be viewed as a traitor. The purpose of this secret mission is to look around, and possibly meet some of the POWS. She is even taught a secret eye-blinking code. Basically, she is asked to put her body where her mouth is. Davee agrees. She knows her life is on the line. She knows how she will be viewed. She knows she can never tell anyone of her role. She knows if she does no one will believe her, our government will deny such involvement, and morally she could put the POWS in more danger.

Ultimately she is dropped from the mission; Davee reads that Jane Fonda has gone to Hanoi. She wonders if the movie-star activist was chosen instead and that rather than Jane Fonda being "Hanoi Jane-a-traitor," she is actually an American hero?

Personally, I believe that such a possibility exists. I have great respect for Jane Fonda and her special brand of integrity as well as that of her husband Tom Hayden. Whether I am on target again remains to be seen. Only history will tell. However, I do believe that if Jane Fonda had been asked to put her body where her mouth was, she would have done it. If you think this is a farfetched idea, ask yourself this: how did an ordinary citizen end up in Hanoi during the war? Could you or I have so casually gone? If what I believe is true, then Jane Fonda is in a Catch-22 position: if she told the truth no one would believe her. Our government could not back her up. Perhaps we shouldn't cast stones so quickly. History may indeed prove that Jane Fonda is truly an American hero which says events may not always be as they appear.

Without going too far off track as far as ORION is concerned, it does appear that I have a good record of capturing contemporary events *prior* to their happening or *prior* to the public's awareness of them.

I do not consider myself a psychic.

Still, I believe in the existence of a sixth sense—intuition, whatever one chooses to call it. I have also found that all human beings have creative abilities, whether it be in music, poetry, cooking or art. Sometimes I am shocked at what I write, particularly when it comes to pass, yet I am not amazed by it.

I have been educated about the levels of the mind, the Alpha level being the most creative, the most physically connected with the universe. Anyone who has ever created anything knows what I am talking about. At the Alpha level you become so totally involved that "time flies"—it is a joyful experience. As for me during the creation of ORION, I always felt "the novel wrote itself."

Without sermonizing, I have always believed in a Higher Power—God—Whomever you conceive this Universal Oneness to be. My relationship with my own soul and that of a Higher Being is personalized. I do not flaunt it or sell it or market it or make it into a law. I do not brag about it or declare my perceptions are the only perceptions, that my way is the only way. My knowledge of the Infinite is but a decimal of the Truth.

More than one person has pointed out that I share the same birthday as the psychic Edgar Cayce, March 18th. I have been tested in front of many authorized witnesses and proven to be "highly sensitive." My inner mind is vulnerable to outside energies, suggestions, moods. I personally believe that no matter how developed our energized component is, all life is part of the same universe and its laws. I believe we share on one level or another both a universal energy and a higher energy.

I was at an all-time energized high when I created ORION. Being in touch with my own soul I felt its soul. I definitely was in touch with something. Under most circumstances I would back away from this sort of personal revelation. I've seen too much victimization perpetuated in the name of religion to infringe my philosophies and beliefs on anyone else. Still, because so much of what I had written has materialized, this element has to be touched upon.

During the creation of ORION a part of me *felt* Elvis had not died. However, since I believe in eternal life, since I believe in the existence of the soul beyond the physical, I must question whether my feelings of Elvis still living simply related to the spiritual existence rather than the physical existence?

"I am, and I was," Elvis said during his final concert tour. Was he trying to tell us something?

124

"The Impossible Dream"
—Elvis Presley Song—1972

TREASURES

Elvis was a prisoner of his fame. To escape his adoring fans, he would have to leave his mansion late at night, often in disguise, often hidden in the trunk of a car. Red and Sony West were recorded as saying that one of the reasons Elvis changed cars so often was that there was so little outside his work and personal environment to interest him. He suffered long bouts of boredom.

It's difficult to envision a man who performed before massive crowds and drove his audience into a frenzy—one of the most recognized faces in the world, so bored that even the most minute problem gave him an excuse to hold a summit meeting. Yet that seems to be the story.

Elvis Presley was a king in exile.

For too long he was unable to serve the masses while at the same time he hungered to do so. Restlessness, anger, boredom took their toll. It's not difficult to understand why he used pills to anesthetize such a high energy level, enabling him to endure. Locked in his bedroom suite, he ate, watched television, read and slept, overindulging in each, which turned into a Catch-22 situation: the overindulgence sapped his energy, made him lazy, overweight and no doubt disappointed in himself. For the most part he did not want his fans to see him in such condition, which must have set into motion inner frustrations, which in turn egged on the urge for more anesthetization. Yet Elvis, more than once, drastically and suddenly turned his situation around. By dieting and working

125

out, the prince frog turned into the king by the kiss of sheer will power.

Elvis Presley *could* meet any challenge.

Once a certain challenge was met, he sought a higher one. He was bored with the type of movies he felt forced to make, bored with having to sing the same old songs at concerts, often complaining that no one listened to the lyrics of his songs. Even though he held great affection for his longtime associates and friends, there had to be that element of boredom which gives way to the dictum, "Familiarity breeds contempt."

It was difficult to make new friends. Who should he trust? Would they like him for himself or for the image? And what about safety? Far too often came the death threats, the threats to kidnap or harm members of his family. He must have questioned often, "Was it worth being Elvis Presley?" Was it worth being buried alive? Had Graceland turned into a gilded mausoleum?

It's not surprising that he began questioning the purpose of his existence. Finding fame so early in life, Elvis' search began at an early age—a continual search for new philosophical ideas and thoughts, an insatiable appetite toward discovering a connection with his higher self as well as the higher selfs relationship with the universe and God. Elvis absorbed and breathed these ideas and could not get enough of them. Yet once they were thoroughly absorbed, he found it challenging to share those ideas. I believe that if Elvis is leading a second life, it is in the field of healing and helping.

We know he spent years emersed in spiritualism, which emphasizes that the spirit is the prime element of reality. To that end he sought a musical outlet to express his total being. The album HOW GREAT THOU ART was a result of this attempt.

It won a Grammy for the best album of the year.

One of the many books which prepared him for the study toward achieving the totalness of his higher self was THE AUTOBIOGRAPHY OF YOGI, where such mysteries as levitation, mental telepathy, materialization and dematerialization are discussed.

It is the study of *complete mind over body*.

The ultimate feat for the life of yogi was the leaving of it.

126

According to one brochure, "No physical disintegration was visible in his body even twenty days after death. No indication of mold was visible on the skin; no odor of decay emanated from his body . . ."

Elvis spoke of this often while continuing his quest and studies of Yoga, which basically seeks to liberate the individual from the illusory world of phenomena and from the cycle of rebirth. The goal of every yogi is to achieve a state of samadhi, or the dissolution of the personality, which is the first step toward knowledge of the absolute. Elvis Presley could not remain Elvis Presley if he sought such liberation.

The shedding of the "old skin for the new" is taken more literally by some. Some philosophies stress that in order to achieve nirvana the individual must place himself in a state of oblivion, one outside the physical reach of pain and suffering.

Personally, I believe that's the easy way "out." As long as we have chosen the physical body on a physical plane of temporary existence, we have to work with it. The physical body is a burden. All of us seek to be the butterfly while living as the caterpillar. Still, the caterpillar must complete its existence before transformation is possible. It's the impatient ones who enter into this state prematurely.

Nature is not impatient. Sometimes man is. Elvis Presley was not known for having patience. This state of impatience and unhappiness with physical conditions could have left him vulnerable to the various philosophies. If he has chosen a new name and another life while still existing physically on this plane, I believe he'll work through such beliefs, eventually coming to term that he *is* Elvis Presley for a reason. (Elvis would never have left this life by suicide as it was against his beliefs.)

If Elvis did hoax the death of "Elvis Presley" in order to become the butterfly, it would be helpful to have total mind control over his body, to be able to go in and out of a self-induced trance, to make his heartbeat inaudible, to control breathing and body temperature. Since training is not done alone but with the assistance of aides, Elvis studied at a spiritual academy located on a mountaintop overlooking Pasadena under the guidance of a woman who called herself Daya Mata. (Daya Mata was the name for a woman fomerly of Salt Lake City.) Taking a "new identity" apparently is part of transformation. Thus it is not difficult to believe that Elvis might choose to live under another name. Not only did Elvis embrace the theories of a higher life, but he found solace in the academy's Meditation Gardens. So impressed was he that he may have duplicated these gardens at Graceland where the shrine with his misspelled name lies.

One of the first things Elvis asked of his spiritual leader was the power to "materialize" and "dematerialize" at will.

Was this a necessary training for the future?

This was achieved through the training of yoga which is divided into eight stages:

The first and second stages are the practice and unfailing observance of moral virtues. (This would mean cleansing of the physical body, nonviolence and a period of chastity.)

The third and fourth stages include the practice of certain difficult and arduous bodily postures and control of the breath, which may include breathing through either nostril at will and retention of the breath for periods up to half an hour (and longer in the more accomplished student, which Elvis was said to have been).

The fifth stage is restraint, in which sense organs are trained to take no notice of their perceptions. (Trance.)

The sixth stage is steadying the mind and excluding worldly thoughts through concentration on a single object.

The seventh stage is meditation, when fully achieved, becomes the eighth and final stage, samadhi—or release.

Also important are the Yoga of Spells, which teach the continual repetition of magical phrases as a means of **disassociating the consciousness.**

The Yoga of Force teaches physical means including acrobatics as a means of salvation, while the Yoga of Dissolution emphasizes **breath control and meditation and extraordinary physical endurance.**

The most important achievement toward salvation and perfection involves the renunciation of worldly attachments and the **SELF.** (If Elvis left using this training, he left behind many worldly goods, including ELVIS PRESLEY.)

Not long before August 16, 1977 Elvis said to Felton Jarvis, his friend and producer at RCA, "You know, Felton, I'm sick and tired of being Elvis Presley . . ."

Faking unconsciousness, even pretending to be dead, was a

128

trick Elvis had used several times prior to August 16th. According to Red West there was a time when Elvis was performing and he began to look sick. Staggering offstage, he collapsed. He was taken to the hospital where the doctors told everyone to leave Elvis and return to the motel to await word, Red writes in his book ELVIS: WHAT HAPPENED? Continuing he says, "They would give us a report as soon as they could. We thought maybe he was dying from some mystery disease." Red relates they all sat around waiting for the worst. Then around one in the morning there was a knock at Red's door. "Damn, man, if it ain't that old sonofabitch Elvis standing their healthier than a herd of cattle, and he is grinning from ear to ear. Not a doggone thing wrong with him. We all pump him full of questions, and he tells us he is now okay. But when the other boys return to their rooms, Elvis makes a confession to me. The whole collapsing routine was just a big act . . ."

Red also mentions another time. "I remember," says Red, "one time we were in a hotel in Colorado, and he (Elvis) called my room and told me to come see him, that there was something he wanted to talk to me about. Well, I got straight to his room and Elvis is lying out of it on the floor. I thought, oh well, he just whacked himself out with something. So I undressed him and put him in bed and covered him up. But later I got to thinking. When he spoke to me on the telephone, he was completely straight, like he hadn't taken a thing, and I got to that room in less than a couple of minutes. Now no drug hits you that hard. So then I suspected that he wasn't asleep or out of it at all. He was wide awake and just faking it, just to see how I would handle him. *He tested us a lot of times like that.*"

Stories such as these, told by many of Elvis' Memphis Mafia make even the most naive wonder if Elvis was ever as "whacked" out as later reported? This could have easily been a method of putting to practice the theory of mind-over-body, and a means of eavesdropping on those close to him, checking their loyalty, listening to what was being said about him. One of Elvis' friends mentions that such a thought crossed his mind.

It is apparent Elvis could use his body as a decoy—that at will he could make his physical condition appear to be other than what was supposed. The question is, how *often* did Elvis practice this? Could he have heard conversations while in that condition—conversations that may have led to the firings of close friends rather than the reported payroll reduction reason?

Only a few years prior to his "death" there was another faked death episode. This not only involved Red and Sonny West but also J.D. Sumner and the Stamps Quartet. The plot was to tell J.D. Sumner and his group that a madman was after Elvis with a gun. To put the plan into motion three security guards were recruited. "We decided," says Red, "to act out a fake gunfight with an assassin." Red continues to describe this incident in the book ELVIS: WHAT HAPPENED? Sonny was to be the assassin with a gun loaded with blanks. He would remain hidden. Everyone, including the security guards emptied their guns and loaded them with blanks, telling J.D. that a madman was loose. "Well, we are up in the suite and J.D. is checking inside doors and his boys are pretty nervous about what's coming down." Sonny soon left on an excuse, leaving J.D. Sumner and the Stamps by the bar talking to Elvis and the security guards. Soon Sonny, who had snuck back in, reached around a corner and started shouting and firing away, with Red shooting back, then staggering and falling "dead." Red says the next fusillade of shots cut down the security guards. It appeared to be a mass slaughter, with those "in on it" falling dead. Those not in on it were hysterical, running, shouting, screaming, hiding. J.D. even threw himself over Elvis' prone body. When it became clear—after Elvis began to laugh convulsively—that the whole faked death scene was just that, J.D. and his group remained understandably terror-stricken.

Red makes a point of saying they could have won Oscars.

It would be well to make a point here that shortly before 1977 Elvis told J.D. Sumner and other members of his entourage that he wouldn't be performing as much the following year as he had been and that they should look for other work. Some people questioned Elvis as to what he actually meant? But he just stood by his statement: "Look for other work."

Elvis had begun to clean house—for this was about the same time he fired Red and Sonny West, and Dave Hebler. All had been with him for years with Red going all the way

130

back to high school. Little by little, one by one, the Memphis Mafia was to be no more.

Red, Sonny and Dave never understood why? And since it was well recognized that Elvis was a born planner, it just wasn't making any sense.

What was happening? Dee and Vernon Presley were no longer a marital team. Linda Thompson (Elvis' girlfriend after his divorce from Priscilla) was no longer around.

It was obvious Elvis Presley was making major changes in his life, that his plans were both secret and surprising. What was not obvious was why?

Many biographers talk about the fact that Elvis Presley possessed an uncanny sense of timing—almost perfection. Elvis chalked this up to having studied numerology. Certain events would be successful if enacted at a particular time. That's why August 16, 1977 was the perfect day. But he also knew that in order for one thing to happen, you must do something else first.

August 16, 1977 was not the end of Elvis Presley. Elvis Presley *is* the cause of Elvis Presley—the persona, the mystique, the uniqueness. Elvis became the "Elvis" he wanted to become. It would be in total character if that "Elvis" was no longer appealing to pull a reverse—to "unElvis" himself.

Living as two-people-in-one began when he was born a twin, a twin he believed to be identical, a part of him that died before having a chance at life. Major studies have been done on twins and their amazing bonding. Even twins separated at birth and without knowledge of such a twinship go through life "in search of" and with a feeling of having a "part of them" missing. That's a credible feeling particularly in the case of identical twins who are created from one egg which divides into two identical halves. This recalls a conversation in which Orion the singer (whichever Orion it was) spoke about the identical twin issue:

"Identical twins come from one egg," Orion had said. "At the moment of conception there is just One Soul, but then the egg divides and becomes two people. Now I believe the soul divides also, each half going into a different body. If one of those identical bodies dies at birth, I believe the soul of the dying twin goes back into the living twin's body—

131

which means the living twin will have twice the talent, twice the fame, yet twice the sorrow, twice the pain."

This conversation plays over and over in my mind, particularly because it occurred long before most of the biographical books on Elvis were released—books which not only emphasized the deep sense of loss Elvis felt about his missing twin but also how Elvis felt completely comfortable leading a double life.

Many of the Elvis biographers have discussed his twin feeling of being both "powerful" and "powerless." On the one hand he had, as Elaine Dundy wrote in ELVIS AND GLADYS, dominated over death. He was the one to survive while at the same time had been powerless to save his brother. He probably harbored guilt. He had lived. Jesse Garon had not.

Elvis, like most of us growing up in the forties and fifties, found his imagination fired by the comic book and radio heroes of the day. Many of these comic book heroes possessed double identities: Clark Kent by day, Superman by night. When I think of the singer Orion and his mask, I am reminded that many of the comic book heroes Elvis admired also wore masks.

Coincidence?

If there were two Orions, each with a mask, then the deception spills over into my life. I do know that at least one Orion is a man named Jimmy Ellis. But the other?

This truth is extensively researched and underscored in ELVIS AND GLADYS where it tells of Elvis' "twin-fusion" with Captain Marvel, Jr. Marvel was a hero on the one hand, but on the other hand lived a normal life as the meek Freddy Freeman. Elvis was so captivated by this comic book hero that it was Captain Marvel, Jr. "who sculpted Elvis' authoritative stance, legs exultantly wide apart, the graceful gestures of his hands, palms flat, fingers outstretched, thumbs extended. It was Captain Marvel, Jr. who styled Elvis' glistening hair, side-parted with the forelock falling over his brow, the sideburns, the hair growing down his neck. Much later would come Elvis' Captain Marvel, Jr. cape and lightning bolt emblems on TCB (Taking Care of Business) and TLC (Tender Loving Care) jewelry."

The lightning bolt displayed on the tail of Elvis' private

airplane, the LISA MARIE, is almost identical to the lightning bolt used in the Captain Marvel, Jr. series. The costume, the cape, the stance depicted Elvis Presley in comic book form.

Rich Stanley says it was the "little boy in him coming out that made him want to be a crusader against evil, like Captain Marvel . . ."

With a double identity as Freddy Freeman, Captain Marvel, Jr., could lead a normal day-to-day existence. As Captain Marvel, Jr. he could fight crime and help make the world safer. To prove my point, I suggest reading the many biographies written since Elvis' "death." All too often stories are repeated:

> Elvis was fascinated with the police. On one occasion he attended a funeral dressed in a police captain's uniform. On yet another occasion he wore a police captain's uniform to a Memphis recording session. He collected badges, emblems, guns, and authoritative identification.

> He became friends with law enforcement divisions and was said to be obsessed with the type of authority a badge or uniform gave. He was known to go out on "drug busts" with the police in squad cars and unmarked cars. One time he disguised himself in a padded jumpsuit while wearing a ski mask.

> And the grand coup of all: going to the White House and into the Oval Office and having President Richard Nixon appoint Elvis Presley a Special Agent of the Bureau of Narcotics and Dangerous Drugs. (December 21, 1970)

Elvis apparently relished being able to have a second and secret life, a life unknown to those even closest to him. Maria Columbus, co-president of THE ELVIS SPECIAL and a special consultant on this project, put out the following news bulletin:

> "While conducting research for our book ELVIS IN PRINT we have written hundreds of letters since 1981. These were written to fans, photographers, professional writers, and businesses. So it hasn't been unusual for us to uncover

a little-known photograph or fact during this time. But the most unusual and very startling information has come from Washington D.C. itself. We are quoting directly from correspondence received from the Department of the Treasury, and Bureau of Alcohol, Tobacco and Firearms.

"During the period of 1974 through 1976, Mr. Presley provided one of our undercover (narcotics) agents, who was a musician, a job cover. Mr. Presley confirmed to anyone inquiring that the agent/musician was a member of one of his traveling bands. Although Mr. Presley was not actively involved in any of the investigations, his assistance in this regard made it possible for our agent to develop a number of quality investigations.' "

Elvis was presented with a Certificate of Appreciation by the Bureau of Alcohol, Tobacco and Firearms by the Regional Director of BATF in 1976. This certificate can be seen on display in the Trophy Room at Graceland.

Further information reveals, "We cannot identify the agent involved, who is not willing to elaborate on his undercover role. Most of the files are criminal investigative files and do not mention or involve Mr. Presley. The fact is Mr. Presley was not aware of these investigations. All he knew was that our agent needed a cover story. Elvis confirmed that our agent was a member of his traveling band. Records do not indicate who initiated the contact between Elvis and the agent."

Let me repeat that last statement: "Records do not indicate who initiated the contact between Elvis and the agent."

What does this signal? Elvis Presley was connected and working in at least one capacity undercover. We know he was appointed Special Agent by the President of the United States years earlier. Thus, he had to have contact, perhaps often. We also know that Special Agents are sometimes given a new identity which would include new driver's license, passport and the like. In the case of Elvis, his code name was John Burrows. If you recall John Burrows is the name the reservation clerk at the Memphis airport said was used by a man bearing a strong resemblance to Elvis Presley the day after Elvis was supposed to have died.

This John Burrows had picked up a ticket for Buenos Aires.

Elvis, therefore, had the means to "unElvis" himself, to very easily slide into a new identity, an identity aided by the government. His being a Special Agent was not a token gesture.

Elvis Presley was Captain Marvel, Jr. and . . . John Burrows was Freddy Freeman. Elvis was a "free man" at last, or was he?

Names were important to Elvis, and the name John was a favorite (John Baron was the name Priscilla and he had chosen had Lisa been a boy. Baron also had the name "aron" as part of it. A fan pointed out to me that Priscilla's new son Navarone also has "aron" as part of it). It is understandable why he would use this name if he is alive.

In addition to Elvis' interest in the comic book image, syndicated columnist Bob Greene, announced that Elvis Presley Enterprises, Inc. had hired an illustrator and author to produce a daily comic strip featuring Elvis as the hero. The idea is that Elvis would have a whole new life as a wholesome and palatable comic strip figure.

Bob Greene quotes one of the attorneys for the estate as saying, "The cartoon strip was conceived as telling the story of Elvis' career, emphasizing the positive. We want to play up the contribution his music has made on Western society." The strip traces the upbeat aspects of Elvis' career: his beginnings, his rise to fame, his Army hitch, movies.

I understand that three weeks' worth of strip have been put together and is with a newspaper syndicate.

It appears that no dream is out of reach for Elvis.

What does this all add up to?

First, there is the personality element of Elvis. From childhood on he fashioned himself as both a superman and a mortal—Captain Marvel, Jr. vs Freddy Freeman.

He was a man who sought one unorthodox challenge after another—a man with an unusual appetite—a man who related with Jesus, with being a savior—a man extremely kind and generous.

As Jerry Hopkins notes in ELVIS: THE FINAL YEARS, "Elvis was the Lone Ranger, giving great gifts and then riding away in his Cadillac." According to close friends Red and Sonny West, as time went on, Elvis treated money with contempt and continually sought innovative ways to give it away. It got to the point that people around him had to be careful not to mention their need for anything, lest Elvis fulfill that need, immediately.

This type of overspending is not only an example of boredom, but I believe that in Elvis' case he felt guilty about having so much. His religious beliefs found no virtue in having money. He was just as happy with collecting a piece of "junk" as he was with items of enormous value, which is displayed in the decor at Graceland. "The actual amounts of his money mattered less and less to Elvis over the years," Rick Stanley (Elvis' stepbrother) wrote in ELVIS: WE LOVE YOU TENDER. "Elvis spent money for fun, to make other people happy, because he was bored, to freak people out . . ."

The Stanley brothers agree Elvis was grateful for his money and worked hard for it, but that "he was also capable of losing all conception of its meaning, taking it for granted, or holding it almost in contempt." And there was a Biblical belief in the karmic cause and effect of money. "Elvis gave," says Rick, "and the Bible says that what you give you get back tenfold. The Bible told him that it was harder for a rich man to enter the Kingdom of Heaven, and Elvis thought about that quite a bit. He tried never to love money or things for their own sake, and often thought of the Biblical adage, 'He that trusteth in his riches shall fall.' "

Thus, the leaving of wealth and a way of life would not have bothered Elvis but would have freed him and would ultimately allow him into heaven.

With his religious beliefs together with his comic book attraction, we then see Elvis' fascination with numerology: August 16, 1977 would be the one day that would fit into his plans to have another identity, another life.

To put this plan into action would require extensive planning:

Get rid of as many people as possible at the mansion. Clean house, (which he did).

Plan a tour to begin the day chosen as a symbolic beginning and end. It would also achieve a secondary purpose: keeping Graceland clutter-free of musicians and friends. Only a handful would remain.

By having a concert tour planned, there would be an excuse to have records, albums and souvenirs available.

Fake a death using mind-over-body control—a practiced past accomplishment.

Have a wax figure in an air-conditioned coffin put on display to prove that Elvis Presley no longer existed.

Commit no fraud. No insurance should be collected, no legal documents left behind to indicate a death had occurred.

Be prepared in case of an emergency—such as moving gravesites to Graceland. This will prevent bodies being exhumed or kidnapped.

Do not tempt fate. Spell name incorrectly on gravesite.

If you tired of one identity, use another. You could always wear a mask.

This is all supposition, of course. Still, if I were to write a script, this would be a way for it to happen.

Fantasy?

Perhaps.

"When I was a boy," Elvis Presley said in 1971, "I was the hero of the comic books and movies. I grew up believing in a dream. Now I've lived it out."

THE COMPLETION

Go for it.
Take it to the max.
Give it hell.
Don't let nothin' stop you.
Take it to the limit.

These are a few of the many expressions Elvis Presley used, expressions that accentuated the dream of a man who refused to operate within the confines of a non-extremist.

Family members state that Elvis was a superstar even when he wasn't onstage and was a showman in everything he did. He was a man who embraced his myths and legends and made them a natural role for himself. He became the myth. He became the legend.

This showmanship was exhibited in various ways. When Elvis dressed, he overdressed. When he ate, he overate. One ring was not enough. One airplane led to many airplanes. There were numerous cars, each driven at top speed. His stepbrother Rick Stanley has said that the ultimate challenge for Elvis was to look death in the eye and grin. He would take everything to the max, just to see if it could be done.

Elvis possessed an insatiable need for a challenge that once met was tossed aside. Confident he could do anything (this was the same man who, without warning, was able to meet with the President of the United States), it falls within the parameters of his thinking that the ultimate challenge of his life could be "the leaving of it."

Elvis was known to destroy at a whim. One such incident involved a small wooden three-bedroom house at the northeast corner at Graceland. Red West tells a story of how Elvis suddenly got it into his mind to wipe that house off the face of the earth. There was nothing wrong with the house. But Elvis had it bulldozed to the ground.

As he was able to destroy the cottage, one wonders if he carried that type of thinking into personal life—the destruction of an identity.

. . . and to repeat what Merle Haggard said in 1979 in PEOPLE MAGAZINE: "Elvis may have faked his death. It would be the first chance for freedom in his entire life—and it could have been a scheme Colonel Parker dreamed up."

Just as mystique surrounds the life and "death" of Elvis Aron Presley, thus is Colonel Thomas Andrew Parker's existence shrouded in mystery. Did the man who orchestrated the "life" of Elvis Presley also orchestrate the "death" of Elvis Presley? Would he have the know-how to remove from Elvis one identity and replace it with another?

According to reports he possessed that type of know-how.

There's a lengthy portrait of the Colonel in Albert Goldman's book ELVIS stating that Tom Parker is in reality Andre van Kuijk. Rather than being born on June 26, 1909 in Huntington, West Virginia, the Colonel was born in the Catholic city of Breda in southern Holland. (No record of the Colonel's birth exist in the files in Huntington, West Virginia.)

Apparently the Colonel was even at an early age masterful in the creation of a new identity. It is said he entered the United States illegally. Regardless, it does appear that he was able to completely disassociate himself with his family and friends back in Holland and mastermind a new life as Colonel Tom Parker of the United States.

His word was golden. Because of this he was able to dispense with many of the legal customs of business. His signature is rarely found on contracts or checks. It is said he has never owned a credit card, pays for everything in cash, and has no passport.

A passport requires proof of birth.

If one were here illegally, it would be well-advised never to appear in a court of law or allow yourself to be the target of legal investigation. The business the Colonel chose to be

139

involved in is fraught with litigation, yet he has managed to stay out of court.

Recently Parker was removed by the probate court from handling Elvis' estate, a result of allegations of mismanagement. The allegations were filed by Lisa's court-appointed guardian. Judge Joseph W. Evans wrote in a heated opinion that, "The compensation received by Colonel Parker is excessive and shocks the conscience of the court." Evans then ordered the Presley estate to cease all dealings with Parker. This same article, which appeared in PEOPLE MAGAZINE, 1981, further states that the Colonel, "rather than being Thomas Andrew Parker from West Virginia is in fact Andreas Cornelis van Kuijk from Breda, Holland who came to the United States in 1929 at the age of 20." The speculation that his is an illegal entry is underlined by PEOPLE's next statement: "His foreign birth supports speculation that the reason Presley never accepted multimillion-dollar overseas gigs was Parker's inability to secure a U.S. passport."

Even Elvis stated once that he thought "the Colonel was born in Holland . . . and that he probably got here by jumping ship."

More than one person who knew the Colonel was to remark that the Colonel had a fear of crossing outside the United States borders and maintained a secret and fictitious past.

The sum total of what the various writers have found out about the Colonel are consistent:

Refused to leave the United States for overseas travel.

Always **overpaid** the IRS, thus avoiding legal investigation.

Avoided being in the position to sue or be sued, thus never being in court.

Operated in cash, thus never authorizing any credit investigation.

Remained secretive and cagey about his past.

I think it's an interesting choice of words which Albert Goldman uses in ELVIS when describing the Colonel: "he made a decision to **inter his past and cover his traces permanently.''**

The unusual business arrangements which existed between the Colonel and Elvis have always been suspicious. According to Memphis attorney Blanchard E. Tual, appointed by the probate court to represent Lisa, Elvis signed away an incredible one-half of his gross to the Colonel, a cut Tual says was "exorbitant, excessive, and unreasonable . . . and raises the question of whether Parker has been guilty of self-dealing." (PEOPLE, 1981)

Not intending to dissect the Colonel and his business dealings, I do believe it is essential to show that if Elvis were to bury his old identity and to establish a completely new life, Colonel Tom Parker possessed such expertise. Because of possibly establishing a new identity and a new life for himself, the Colonel's family thought him dead. The Colonel has always managed to divert any serious attention directed at him. He is definitely a "now you see me, now you don't" enigma.

People near the Colonel said he did not act surprised by the death of Elvis. He had taken Elvis into his company Boxcar Enterprises and instead of going to Memphis on August 16th, he flew to New York to meet with Harry Geissler, owner of Factor's, a merchandising firm that has put out collectables such as the Farrah Fawcett tee-shirts. The Colonel signed a deal for the merchandising rights to Elvis that in "death" would be worth millions.

I find it interesting to note that this deal with Factors was negotiated by the Colonel and Boxcar Enterprises rather than the Presley Estate. Apparently the Colonel and his associates received seventy-five percent of this merchandising income— again, an incredible amount. Goldman points out in his investigative book that there was a ten percent off-the-top "finder's fee" commission paid to the William Morris Agency!

William Morris again? Not only had I learned of the close relationship between the Colonel, Abe Lastfogel and Bob Neal but Albert Goldman in his ELVIS pointed out that some of the salary of the Colonel's large staff was actually paid for by the William Morris Agency.

Goldman points out that Abe Lastfogel, the president of William Morris, was the mouthpiece for Colonel Parker.

141

With this kind of closeness, I have to question the type of deals which were made on behalf of and for Elvis Presley. I wonder just how self-serving these deals were? But more, why had these same people at William Morris courted me? And then when I did not play ball, why was my novel ORION stopped? Why suddenly did this piece of fiction disappear from every shelf across the United States—a novel that shows step-by-step how a superstar man of song hoaxes his own death, with the help of his manager and doctor, and a small group of family and friends! Was all of this simply coincidence? Just because my novel seemed to be coming true, written prior to many events being recorded in book or the media, did I really have any evidence that the Colonel's buddies and the Colonel wanted ORION stopped? Just because the Colonel's buddies were with William Morris and the same top people both wrote and telephoned me should be listed as coincidence, shouldn't it? And just because my former editor told a top literary agent that it was rumored that the Colonel had ORION stopped, I should, again, chalk it up to coincidence, should I? Yet:

ORION was here one day, gone the next.

I was paid a hefty advance and told to keep the money.

I was instructed never to mention Elvis Presley in connection with ORION.

I was courted by letters and telephone calls by all three offices of the William Morris Agency: Nashville, New York and Los Angeles. At least two of these were top powers at William Morris and also close friends with the Colonel.

I received late night telephone calls from a mystery voice calling himself Orion. Yet I discovered it was not the same Orion as Jimmy Ellis, ironically on the SUN RECORDS label, Elvis' old label.

Because ORION was declared fiction, because I had always made it clear that it was not an imitation of the life of

Elvis Presley and because I never said Elvis was alive, there was never any litigation to stop me. From what has been reported about the Colonel, he doesn't like courts of law. It would have been much easier to have been stopped legally. I could have fought back.

Whatever was done was done quietly.

I can't believe ORION was pulled because it was not worthy. There is a great deal of documentation in the form of letters from agents, publishers and movie producers to support my belief that ORION was a good book. Thus I have to ask repeatedly: was ORION stopped because it unwittingly described how a superstar of song hoaxed his death? Was this novel too close to the truth for comfort? Would it have been taken seriously if there had not been independent media attention as to why there was a cover-up in the death of Elvis Presley? (Such as ABC's 20/20.)

More than one person has made comments about my personal safety in connection with revealing what happened to me: the novel ORION and its connections, the singer who took his identity from the novel, truths uncovered, rumors explored, the presentation of a mystery tape, where Elvis is living (if he is living) and under what name.

I can't be worried about my safety. I certainly have no cause for alarm from anyone at William Morris. There were never any threats. In fact I want to stress that the Morris people were always polite and supportive. I truly liked Bob Neal and Mel Berger when we met. I never met Abe Lastfogel but he was gentle on the telephone. And when Mae Axton originally asked me to sign an autographed copy of ORION for the Colonel, she said his reaction to the novel was to chuckle. The only way I found out anything was to have some insiders investigate. That's how I discovered that it appeared ORION was indeed a victim. And although the "death" of Elvis was most assuredly unprofitable as far as ORION went, the death definitely improved business for the Elvis industry:

Approximately 2,000 visitors a day visit Graceland, 700,000 annually. The 10th Anniversary drew 50,000.

Graceland brings in 9 million dollars a year, making Elvis' home one of the most successful tourist attractions in the world, and it has become the most recognizable private home in America, second only to the White House. It takes a staff of approximately 100–400 people (many part-time) to manage Graceland.

Elvis made more than 900 recordings, including 140 million-selling gold records. **In all, his records have sold more than 1 billion copies—half of them since his death!**

Merchandising of Elvis memorabilia brings in more millions as do the Collector's items. For example, the first five records Elvis made for Sun Records sold in 1955 for 89 cents. In 1977, a set of five Sun Records sold for $4,000.

There are about 200 Elvis fan clubs in the United States, some with over 3,000 members. There are more than 50 fan clubs overseas and new ones starting every year. The largest fan club is in Great Britain which claims 20,000 members and publishes a monthly magazine. England has at least 27 tribute magazines.

Clubs, fans and the fans at large are petitioning the United States government to honor Elvis Presley with a national holiday or, at least, a postage stamp.

The study of Elvis Presley has become a requested course in some universities.

Magazines and newspapers universally report that when they feature a cover story on Elvis Presley their circulation and sales increase significantly. THE NATIONAL ENQUIRER went from six million to seven million on a featured Elvis story. THE STAR reports a 46% increase. THE COMMERCIAL APPEAL in Memphis reported selling 323,000 additional copies to their normal 250,000 the day Elvis died.

Books written about Elvis sell in the millions and continue to enjoy a long shelf life.

Elvis Presley has one of the most recognizable faces in the world. He may be the only person who was known worldwide by his first name! One story tells of a reporter having gone to a rural part of Africa only to discover in a makeshift hut a poster of Elvis Presley.

An English gentleman, upon hearing The King Is Dead, thought, "how sad." When he found out it was Elvis the papers talked about, he flew to Memphis.

In Hamburg, West Germany a poll of 2100 teenagers were asked whom they would most like to emulate: 20% picked their fathers, 17% their mothers, 12% Jesus Christ, 8% Elvis Presley.

It's fascinating that Elvis saw a connection between him and Jesus. They shared the same astrological sign, the same amount of letters in their first name and were both called a "king." (Although Elvis often corrected such terminology by stating, "there's only one King—our Lord.") Elvis' known generosity was based on his Jesus-connection. Although Jesus is considered the great healer, Elvis felt he had a power to heal. Elvis, besides the "laying on of hands," was fascinated with medicine and would sit for hours reading medical manuals, perhaps looking for the way to heal or just satisfying his curiosity as well as combating boredom. On his visits to the funeral parlor late at night to study bodies he would discuss such topics as embalming with knowledge and ease. "If Elvis had not been an entertainer, he might have been a doctor," his stepmother once said.

Not only did Elvis see a connection between himself and Jesus, and I say this in the most respectful sense, but so do his fans. "Pilgrimages are made to his shrine, where his followers kneel in prayer," is the way one newspaper described the fans' visits to Graceland's Meditation Gardens. And according to a recent magazine article, "In the years following Elvis' death, he has become sainted . . ."

Some have been inclined to draw an analogy between Elvis' childhood and that of Jesus: a simple man, born in a small town, who sought a good and pure life. As Catholics view Jesus' mother as holy, so Elvis viewed his mother.

One of the elements in ORION which amazes me still is the Jesus connection. In fact, so much of ORION is symbolic of the story of Jesus in contemporary terms, from the sighting of the star to the Holy Mother theme, as well as the feeling that God was the father of Orion rather than Jess. Keep in mind that ORION was copyrighted in 1978, years *before* biographies such as ELVIS by Albert Goldman revealed Elvis' strong connection with Jesus.

Perhaps that is another reason this novel is unique. I say via fiction and via my hero ORION, that Dixie (which equates to Mary) had a vision and there was an immaculate conception, that Dixie and Orion felt connection but that the father Jess was left out. When I read Goldman's biography years after my book was written, I was astounded to read, "Thus, like the heroes of mythology (remember I created ORION from the combination also), Elvis came to believe that the man he called 'Daddy' was no more **his father than was Joseph the father of Jesus.** Further confirmation of this weird notion was the story Vernon told of going out into the backyard on the night of the birth and being astonished to see the heavens ringed around with a blue light. This recollection thrilled Elvis because blue was a color he had long identified with himself and to which he attributed supernatural significance."

In ORION, written years *prior*, I write of a similar vision:

Kissing the boy's head, Dixie's face again mystically transformed. "When I was a young girl I happened onto something special. It only happened once. The winter sun had set and the sky and earth looked to be on fire, a dying soft fire. I watched for a long time and right before the sky totally blackened, there was this cloud-like sphere linking the heavens with the sun, then something strange took place. Three of the brightest stars I ever seen took form. I thought at first that it was the Holy Father, the Holy Mother and the third, the brightest, the Holy Son." Dixie's eyes misted over with the strange zodiac memory.

"What I had seen, Jess, was the Belt of Orion. Not many people see Orion but I did and when you see it you don't easily forget it. Just once, I saw it just once and try as hard as I might, I never saw Orion again. Yet while it lasted they were the brightest stars in the whole universe, the brightest I ever saw." Dixie's eyes cleared and she touched the baby's face reverently. "I'm going to name my son Orion . . ."

Goldman, as well as other biographers, equate Elvis with the mythical hero. Jesus was from the House of David. My fictional Orion was symbolically from the House of David via my having him live in Nashville—which is in Davidson County. Elvis Presley often compared his profile to that of the Biblical David as well as wearing the Star of David around his neck. Besides the code name of John Burrows, Elvis also used the name of John Carpenter which would have dual significance: Jesus was a carpenter and Dr. John Carpenter was the name of a character Elvis played in the movie CHANGE OF HABIT.

Elvis was a student of the various philosophies and religious theories. I've been told that he read the book THE PASSOVER PLOT with great interest. Since Elvis identified with Jesus, then his reading about what Jesus *might* have done according to THE PASSOVER PLOT might take on another dimension.

Many of Elvis' friends discuss how upset Elvis was about the book ELVIS: WHAT HAPPENED? written by his closest friends. The book hurt Elvis and he told a friend that he knew how Jesus felt when Judas sold Jesus out for a bag of gold. "They are my Judas. They sold me out for a bag of gold . . ."

"I don't believe ELVIS: WHAT HAPPENED? caused Elvis to think about hoaxing his death, but I do believe it more or less substantiated his plans," a fan recently theorized. "If Elvis hoaxed his death, I think the idea was brewing for quite a while. That's why he began to clean house, sell things such as the farm, change his will, divert funds, and make the kinds of necessary arrangements it requires for a new life and a new identity."

Another theory, this one from a newspaper friend, is that since Elvis was a special agent of the Bureau of Narcotics and Dangerous Drugs, he is working undercover as an agent, and that our government provided him with new credentials, even helped orchestrate a cover-up.

"Why would our government become involved?" I questioned.

147

"It's not beyond reason. After all, Elvis was a special agent, perhaps even an undercover agent. His life may have been in danger, who knows?" my friend added.

This gave me food for thought. Elvis did have an undercover agent as a member of his traveling band. No one knows why. Elvis' close friend and sidekick was John O'Grady, formerly with the Los Angeles Police Department's narcotic squad. There is definitely a connection.

Another theory involves the Colonel and his prowess as a hypnotist. Stories abound of how the Colonel could make grown men get down on all fours and act like cats and dogs through the power of hypnotism. Many testify to the amazing ability of the Colonel to employ mind control. There were times when Elvis appeared passive and in a zombie-like condition at meetings. Some swear Elvis was hypnotized. Sonny and Red West recall that the Colonel could do mass hypnosis.

The ability to hypnotize could come in handy if one were to set the scene for a faked death, to make a body appear "zombie-like," and to exert mind control over witnesses.

This is just a theory, of course.

Whether the Colonel orchestrated the "death" of Elvis or not, he did orchestrate the funeral: he hired comedian Jackie Kahane to deliver the eulogy, which to many seemed an odd choice. The Colonel then hired a minister, who was not Elvis or Vernon's minister, to give an address. Third, he hired Rex Humbard, the famed television evangelist. (Elvis supposedly only met Humbard once in a brief backstage meeting.)

While Elvis' body was in view, the Colonel and Vernon Presley were putting together a merchandising package that would bring in millions. Various other contracts were coming to an end. "All in all," one fan newsletter stated, "August 16, 1977 was a convenient time to bring to close the career of one of the most adored men on the planet, while leaving the financial doors wide open." It became immediately clear that Elvis loomed bigger in "death" than he did in "life."

A frequent observation about the Colonel was "he acted as if Elvis had never died," and was heard to say, "Nothing has changed . . ." In fact the famed wheeler-dealer began cutting deals so fast it was mind-boggling, so mind-boggling that in the first year after his "death," Elvis Presley made more money than he had during his entire life.

148

Nobody could have known the extent of loyalty the fans would display. Whether Elvis' "death" gave Elvis a new lease on life is an unanswered question. What is known is that this same "death" brought an unexpected and uncalculated bounty of fortune.

Also under scrutiny was the Colonel's behavior at the funeral. He showed no grief. He said little. He took no part in the ceremony.

For almost two years Vernon Presley and the Colonel ran the growing financial empire of Elvis Presley. Then, ironically on the Colonel's 70th birthday, June 26, 1979, Vernon Presley died. The Colonel's bounty and services soon were halted. A probate judge launched the investigation that would ultimately force the Colonel to sever all connections with the Presley name.

It was done quietly and little is known about the severing arrangements. An era of power had ended.

If Elvis were alive, he was at the starting point again.

THE TRIAL RUN

If Elvis hoaxed his death, Priscilla and Lisa would know about it. Is this one of the reasons Lisa was at the mansion rather than in California? Could this have been a safeguard against being frightened by the news? Many have wondered why, since Elvis was to leave on tour the 16th, Lisa was still at the mansion?

It was one of the longest visits Lisa had made. It seemed out of the norm that Elvis would leave for an extended tour without first seeing that Lisa was safely home with Priscilla.

When Priscilla Presley's book ELVIS AND ME was released in 1985, I read it with great curiosity. The first thing I noted was her special thanks to Norman Brokaw and Owen Laster, both heavyweights with the William Morris Agency, Brokaw in Los Angeles and Laster in New York.

Although I never created Danielle in ORION after Priscilla, but rather from mythology's Danäe, "an only child, beautiful above all women who conceived a child by the god" (Orion being a "god" such as was Elvis sometimes thought of by adoring fans), there is a resemblance. Of course, since ORION was released years prior to Priscilla's book, there was no way I could copy her life nor know how closely she actually resembled the Danäe of mythology. Danäe/Danielle's Dixieland imprisonment, rather than being Priscilla's Graceland gilted cage, was inspired by a quote from Edith Hamilton's book on MYTHOLOGY:

"So Danäe endured, the beautiful,
To change the glad daylight for brass-bound walls,
And in that chamber secret as the grave
She lived a prisoner . . ."

Since Danäe is a young virgin, Orion ultimately meets her in the daylight (Hawaii). Their ultimate marriage brings her to Dixie-Land, "the chamber of the south" which becomes a grave where she lives as a "prisoner."

Danäe/Danielle's escape in ORION (like Orion's) would be to some distant shore. Again from the mythological Danäe:

". . . all around them were the islands and a wave seemed to lift them (Danäe and her child) and carry them swiftly and safely from the sea to shore."

Creating Danielle from mythology fell into line with the mythological Arion who:

". . . lived about 700 B.C. It is said that he had gone from Corinth to Sicily to take part in a music contest as a master of the lyre. He won the great prize and on his voyage home, sailors planned to kill him for it. The god Apollo told Arion in a dream of his danger, and how to survive. When the sailors attacked Arion, he begged a final favor: to let him play and sing once more. At the end of the song, Arion threw himself into the sea where dolphins, enchanted by Arion's music, bore him safely to shore."

Again, the theme of ORION falls under the umbrella of mythology. Orion, in order to survive, sings for the last time, fakes his death and ends up on an island as does Danäe/Danielle.

The next question to be asked in light of the fact the novel ORION "disappeared," is this what happened to Elvis?

It's well documented he was psychic. We know his life was often in danger. He did sing for the last time, and in fact gave many clues that he was about to leave. Did he go to Hawaii? We know he loved Hawaii. And in the mystery tape, which I'll translate shortly, he talks about going to an island.

Yet, again, ORION was creative fabrication, as was Danielle

151

and even Orion's manager/agent Mac Weiman. Without doing the treatise on the creation of the novel ORION at this writing, I do want to point out that Orion's manager was not copied after Colonel Tom Parker but again from a combination of the Bible and mythology. First, Mac was created from Job 9, which unites Orion and the Bear. Second, it fulfilled the prophecy, ". . . who seals up the stars." Basically it is this combination who "offers to Orion the world." Mac (as with mythology) promises to make Orion a god in exchange for his soul. At no time does Mac Weiman represent the word "devil," for in the final analysis Mac possesses a noble soul and a deep sense of love, shown by his sacrificing of himself for Orion. It was this "bear of a man" who would seemingly have the most to lose by the hoaxing of Orion's death. This is illustrated in Orion's final goodbye to the man who originally owned his soul:

"There was one person left for Orion to say goodbye to. That person stood in the near distance, alone. Orion turned and slowly walked toward the great man.

Mac embraced his boy close; for the first time in his life he allowed the tears to run openly and unashamedly down his face. Neither Orion nor Mac could speak.

Danielle also cried without shame. She realized at that moment that there were times when love was so intense that only the heart could speak.

". . . he was shown all the kingdoms of the world and was told, "To you I will give all this authority and their glory; for it has been delivered to me, and I give it to whom I will. If you then will worship me, it shall all be yours." That was taken from Luke 4; it helped create the inner character of Mac Weiman, who possessed the power of the world, a power he promised Orion, a power filled with wealth, a kingdom. Again, I was writing ORION using age-old symbolisms and parables: a Christian possessed by the devil. (So many of the Elvis biographers actually use these descriptions in describing the see-sawing actions of Elvis. But I wrote it first.)

Orion thus spends so much of his mature life battling against overindulgence and sin. Ultimately Orion wins out

152

and redeems his soul. This seemingly also parallels the life of Elvis, but in no way was this meant to imitate it, any more than Elvis deliberately imitated the life of Jesus or that of mythology's Orion/Arion. What is proven is that there is a basic truth to all life and that's probably why I captured "the soul and essence" of Elvis Presley . . . just as Elvis captured the "soul and essence" of all that went before him.

This is only a brief synopsis on how some of the main characters in ORION were created. I realize that not everyone is a student of the Bible and mythology. Still, I found it necessary to do a complete recording of how ORION was created. Perhaps I instinctively knew that this entire project was very unusual and history might welcome this record.

I understandably read Priscilla's book with interest. And I was totally shocked! So much of what she described in 1985 I wrote in 1977 and copyrighted in 1978! Again, I had not imitated life, but life seemed to have imitated my art!

I had no way of knowing Elvis called Priscilla "little one," yet I have Orion calling Danielle by that pet name.

I had no way of knowing that Elvis would ask Priscilla if "she had been good" while he was away, yet I have Orion asking Danielle that same question, using the same term.

Not being privy to their bedroom, I had no way of knowing that Elvis and Priscilla engaged in pillow fights, yet I have Orion and Danielle engaged in one.

I had no way of knowing that Elvis sang HAWAIIAN WEDDING SONG to Priscilla, yet I have Orion singing it to Danielle.

I had no way of knowing that after the birth of their baby, Elvis would not touch Priscilla, that she asked, "why won't you touch me?" Yet I have this exact scene in Orion and have Danielle repeating these same words!

Over and over, almost exactly, scenes and dialogue are repeated. How did I know, having written ORION years before Priscilla's book, about important events? One would have to peruse both books to do this statement justice, but it amazed me. One scene that most amazed me was when Priscilla described an incident which took place toward the end of their marriage. It occurred in a hotel room. Elvis forcibly made love to her. She describes her hurt and the fact she remained awake throughout the night, grieving. It was a reconciliation attempt that had come too late.

Over and over I read what she had written. My God! How can this be? I had written the same thing in ORION. It was also in a hotel room, and their marriage was near its end. My description was more poetic, but still, the "essence" was identical.

> Suddenly, Orion picked up Danielle and carried her into the room, his mouth pressing urgently on hers. His passion shocked and frightened her. They were on the bed, and he was tearing at her clothes, his kisses no longer gentle, but painful. One part of her wanted to scream and run, while another began to respond wildly to his hands and the heat of his body.

> When he took her, it was not as before. There was no tenderness, no words of love, no gentle touch. They were no longer as God had made them, one complete being.

> Inside her tormented soul wept.

> Stunned and unable to sleep, she had spent the rest of the night listening to her husband sleep, afraid to explore the new terror which gripped her mind . . .

I still do not know how I imagined all of these things. Yet Mae also said I knew so much, that I used phrases identical to those his father and mother used. I was only in high school when Elvis' mother died, so I had no way of knowing this family, nor of knowing how they thought or how they spoke. Yet many who knew Elvis and his parents, say I have "locked" into them. If that is true, then it was done on another level of the mind, a level I cannot use at will, but a level that has occurred on other occasions.

The final analysis though is far more startling. Since it has been shown that I "tuned" in to even the most intimate and little known details, then one might guess I had also "tuned" into other incidents, including what became the climax of ORION: **the hoaxing of the death.**

Although I was shocked at how close I had come to real

154

incidents as described in ELVIS AND ME, several other factors surprised me: One is that Priscilla's natural father's last name was Wagner. Wagner is my family name. Priscilla even looks like members of the Wagner family. (It wouldn't shock me to discover we're related, especially after the Mae Axton connection! Nothing relating to ORION should surprise me anymore. But it does.)

The second factor I question is Priscilla's recall of August 16, 1977. She says she heard the news of Elvis' death sometime around noon or shortly after. Noon in California is two o'clock in Memphis. Elvis had not been pronounced dead at two. The body was *about* to be discovered. Giving her benefit of all doubt, let's suppose it was three o'clock in Memphis, and she is notified. She then says she asked that the airplane LISA MARIE be sent for her. It was. In her own words she states she boarded the LISA MARIE around nine o'clock that evening.

Nine o'clock Los Angeles time is eleven o'clock Memphis time.

Priscilla describes the trip as seeming endless. It would have taken around four hours to fly across country. But again, to give all benefit of doubt, suppose the trip was a speed test of three hours. The earliest she could arrive in Memphis would be two in the morning. After the landing was the limousine ride to Graceland. There was a crush of photographers, traffic was heavy. Arrival time at Graceland would be around two thirty in the morning the earliest. Most of the family and close friends were either in Elvis' grandmother's room or in the den.

Except for Lisa Marie, her nine year old child.

She states that Lisa was outside on the lawn riding around on a golf cart given her by Elvis.

It's at least two thirty in the morning—more like three or three thirty. The media and the fans are crushing the gates. There is noise and commotion and thousands of people. There are lights and cameras and cries of disbelief. Yet the one person, a child at that, who need protection is outside riding around in a golf cart!

Priscilla goes on to describe how she took Lisa into her arms and then released her to allow her to ride around in her golf cart again. Why would any nine year old child be allowed outside in the wee hours of the morning? This was not an ordinary child. This was the daughter of Elvis Presley. This was the same child Elvis feared would be the target of kidnapping or harm.

Priscilla's story makes neither rational sense nor maternal sense. What I suspect is Priscilla has her "story" mixed up. Perhaps she was at Graceland all along, or she has not taken care to make sure her story is "pat." There is, even to the most uninformed, an element of disbelief with her version. Many question as to whether it is total fabrication. It is also hard to believe that, with the thousands flocking to Graceland and clogging Elvis Presley Boulevard, if Priscilla had come at that particular hour, she would have found a speedier way to get to Graceland rather than by limousine. Why not a helicoptor? Yet she states she was ushered into a waiting limousine which sped (in all that traffic?) to Graceland.

At the viewing and the funeral Priscilla and Lisa were tremendously composed.

Rethinking the events prior to the "death" takes on wider speculation. It bears repeating. During the three weeks Lisa was at Graceland—Lisa's longest visit since Elvis and Priscilla divorced—Elvis spent a great deal of time with her every day. August 16th arrived. Elvis was leaving for an extended tour. Why hadn't Elvis sent Lisa back to Los Angeles on the LISA MARIE the day before? Why would she still have been at Graceland on the 16th, a day Elvis was unavailable and was "sleeping away?" Lisa had arrived on the LISA MA-RIE. Yet there were no plans to return her. She couldn't have returned on the LISA MARIE on the 16th because it was scheduled to leave for Portland, Maine for the tour. One possible answer, although unlikely, is that the LISA MARIE was headed to Los Angeles, or Las Vegas to pick up members of Elvis' band and take them to Portland, and that Elvis would travel to Portland in the Jet Star. If this is true, then the LISA MARIE should have been on its way for the cross country flight and back. Another theory is that Elvis was planning to have Lisa flown home on a commercial airplane. Again, this would be unusual for Elvis, as he owned several airplanes. Elvis feared for Lisa's safety. He feared kidnapping attempts. This fear could have been eliminated by having Lisa return to California on the 15th. This was not done. Why?

"I believe Elvis wanted Lisa at Graceland so she would be assured her 'daddy was fine,' " is one analysis.

"I think it's possible that Priscilla was secured inside Graceland prior to the death announcement," is another story.

Perhaps there is a good explanation to Priscilla's 'Lisa being outside' story on the night Priscilla arrived—a night etched into the memories of the world—a night when the city of Memphis was in chaos.

Many believe that Priscilla and Elvis were always in love. I believe it. Priscilla said that when she was leaving Elvis they talked about there being "another time, another place."

"He had it all within the palm of his hand," reflects Dee Presley in ELVIS: WE LOVE YOU TENDER. "He had a beautiful wife and a beautiful little daughter that he couldn't be with and I think that hurt him tremendously." Dee says further that "Elvis was the sort of person who didn't readily allow people into his life to begin with, but once he opened to a person to a level where love was possible, that person became a part of his soul—a permanent part of his emotional life. That is what made the loss of Priscilla so hard to take."

(As an aside, had anyone noticed that Priscilla, in her role of Jenna Wade on TV's DALLAS, was the woman who loved Bobby Ewing in an episode centering around Bobby Ewing's return from the dead?)

Many report they have seen and talked to Elvis Presley since August 16, 1977. Carole Halupke and I were told by a songwriter at Mae Axton's home that he had actually run into Elvis in Atlanta.

A Tennessee farmer who knew Elvis swears he saw the superstar outside Graceland seconds before the radio announced Elvis had died.

There have been many television shows with the plot of its hero either faking his or her death, or returning from the dead. One regularly-featured television show with stories to amaze had as its plot a superstar singer who hoaxed his death only to come back as his twin, Jesse Garon, who ends up killing the singer.

According to THE ELVIS SPECIAL, on a Fantasy Island segment Paul Williams played a superstar, complete with jumpsuit, who faked his death to escape from mafia types who were after him.

THE ELVIS SPECIAL also reports that on Showtime Short Subjects there was an animated feature titled "Celebrity," focusing on a superstar named Norm Stern who took a week off from his superstar duties to relax. The world, deciding he was dead, had a funeral. His mansion was turned into a museum tourist attraction. People who knew him wrote books about him, causing Norm to write, under an alias, his own book.

On a T.J. Hooker segment, THE ELVIS SPECIAL says this sentence was mentioned: "Yeah, that girl is as dead as Elvis Presley is supposed to be."

I've heard this remark mentioned carelessly many times. It seems many people believe Elvis may have hoaxed his death.

In his book ELVIS AFTER LIFE Dr. Raymond Moody interviewed a truck driver from a small Alabama town, who described an encounter with Elvis Presley on December 20, 1980 at about nine-thirty at night. The man was about a hundred miles west of Memphis and wanted to visit his mother in Alabama for Christmas. He rarely picked up hitch-hikers. While stopping for fuel and coffee, he noticed a man trying to hitch a ride to Memphis. For some reason, the truck driver trusted the man although he never found out why the man was hitchhiking. On the trip they talked casually, with the man always being polite, saying "Yes, sirs," or "No, sirs." The hitchhiker mentioned he had once been a truck driver, knew a lot about cars and talked of owning several Cadillacs. He had a hat on and it was dark so that the man's face was obscure. The truck driver mentioned he had been having trouble with alcohol, but had quit drinking. The hitchhiker admitted he'd had trouble with painkillers and sleeping pills. Asking to be left off on Elvis Presley Boule-vard, the truck driver told the hitchhiker his name. The hitchhiker turned to him and looked him straight in the eyes and said, "I'm Elvis Presley . . ."

"It was Elvis Presley, all right," the truck driver told Dr. Moody, "or his ghost."

There could be many other explanations for this sighting: delusion, imagination, or the results of being an alcoholic. (This vision has caused the truck driver some mental agony, as it would any of us. Perhaps this book will put his mind at ease. He's not alone in his sightings.)

Countless calls have been received by me and by a business associate from a woman in Michigan. She is a grandmother and never was an avid Elvis fan. Yet she, and others, swear they have seen Elvis in their area in the past year—1987.

"He may have purchased a hotel here," the woman stated. "The hotel sat empty for many years and then was turned into offices. But there's a private residence on an upper level."

She thinks he goes by the name of John Burrows. Across from the hotel is a YWCA where he works out with karate. He's been spotted at a shopping mall, one time with Lisa. "I saw Lisa and Priscilla looking at perfume in a store at the mall," this woman swears. "I know it was them."

Another resident from that small Michigan town called to report a similar sighting. According to at least five people Elvis has been seen at the local mall, at several restaurants, at B. Dalton's Bookstore, the Y, Wendy's, and Burger King. While at a grocery store the man described as looking like Elvis carried a motorcycle helmet, was dressed in a white motorcycle jumpsuit, wore tinted glasses, was not thin but not fat, had his hair cut shorter and rounder with sideburns short showing a touch of grey. At the mall he was spotted wearing a brown leather jacket, pressed jeans, no hat but glasses. Again, his hair was short and rounded. "His face looks the same," this resident says. "When I stared at him he looked nervous, but when I turned to my grandson, he relaxed because he knew I wasn't going to bother him. We're a small community and we leave people alone. Believe me, I wouldn't make this up. And I'm not a liar. You can check up on me. I am certain Elvis Presley is here. Lisa and Priscilla visit. Lisa stayed a while." She then presented me with a telephone number of a man named J. Burrows. "My son called this number and left a message," she swears. "Elvis returned the call. It was his voice. When he realized he didn't know my son, he disconnected."

I tried the number and indeed I was able to leave a message for a John Borrows; it was a hotel complex. I did not receive a call back.

There may be some validity to this woman's story because

of a recent conversation I had with a disc jockey named Doc Varb from Louisville, Kentucky. He has stated openly his belief that Elvis Presley is alive. He also said something else interesting. "I have a well-known singer friend who knows Elvis is alive. He said a few years before Elvis' death, Elvis bought this old hotel . . ."

I had not mentioned to Doc about the Michigan sightings nor about the hotel. If it's a case of mistaken identity then it would be an unnecessary problem for this gentleman. Either way, whoever this J. Burrows is, he is deserving of privacy. (I checked with information in this Michigan town and was told that J. Burrows has a private unlisted telephone number despite the fact I was given a number to call.)

I also refrain from naming many who have said to have seen Elvis Presley since 1977 because of what it does to their reputation. "People think I'm crazy when I say I've seen Elvis," said one songwriter.

As you read this book, you may shrug and say these last few statements sound like they're straight from the check-out line magazines at the supermarket. It's simply that I don't morally believe I need intrude in Elvis' life if he is alive.

It *was* the name "John Burrows" that supposedly came up on a taped talk show which guested Burt Reynolds. There was a live audience phone-in where Burt received a phone call from a soft spoken man who asked Burt how he had been, that it had been awhile since they saw each other and that he hoped to see him soon. Burt sat there with a glazed look and they cut to a commercial. The telephone caller identified himself as "John Burrows."

I've had other reports about Elvis or someone sounding like Elvis calling disc jockeys during the year 1981: there was Jay Albright at KEEN Radio in San Jose, California. I've listened to a taped copy and the voice does sound like Elvis Presley. I believe the caller identified himself as Sivle. In May of 1981 a man named Sivle spoke with Lynn Seman, then Assistant Promotional Director of Station WBAL in Baltimore, Maryland. According to a woman who wrote me, Elizabeth Pierce, she wrote to Ms. Seman who admitted she had talked to someone who sounded like Elvis Presley. During that same month this Sivle also was interviewed by Bill Payne of station KTFX in Tulsa, Oklahoma. That interview was also taped.

A great deal of controversy exists within some fan clubs concerning the identity of Sivle or in some cases, Sivle Nora. The bottom line is no one seems to know *who* Sivle is. I've never spoken to him. I have no idea as to his identity or why he would have called radio stations. Just the fact that these reputable and credible media people could entertain the possibility that it was Elvis Presley calling says something in itself.

While on the subject of disc jockeys, Hugh Jarrett, now with WSB Radio in Atlanta, responded to my request concerning a possible appearance by him on a television program focusing on ORION, as well as this book. Hugh is famous as being one of the Jordanaires, one of Elvis' backup groups. I met Hugh years ago right after ORION was first released. We discussed the novel and Elvis. Unfortunately, Hugh does not recall our meeting or reading ORION. As we talked, a few things clicked into place, but on the whole, Hugh didn't remember most of our meeting. However, I remember it quite well. I found Hugh extremely nice with a gentleman's air about him; he's well thought of in the radio community. When I told him about this book as it related to ORION as well as the possibility that Elvis could be alive, he became very upset and basically said that whoever voiced such a question was totally incorrect, and that he would in no way endorse any project along those lines. I explained that I was now at a disadvantage, since he did not remember me or ORION. I further explained that the program had nothing to do with asking anyone to endorse Elvis being alive but that the program would feature open dialogue.

It became obviously clear that Hugh was against the media asking questions which related to the hoaxing of Elvis' death. "My friend Elvis died," he stressed over the telephone. "It was his body in the coffin."

I thought I had recalled Hugh as saying he did not go to the viewing. "Did you go to Graceland and see the body in the coffin?" I asked.

"No," he stated firmly, "but my friend Felton Jarvis went and he told me it was Elvis in the coffin and he was dead."

Felton Jarvis was Elvis' record promoter from RCA. Songwriter Ray Pennington, recently recounted what he told me years earlier: that he has always believed Elvis to be alive, brought up the name of Felton Jarvis. Secondly, those who saw Felton the day after Elvis' "death," say they were surprised to find him humming and whistling and not at all sad or upset.

If Felton believed Elvis had died, would he have been so cheerful?

I asked Hugh if he thought I had a right to tell my story from my perspective since it was obvious to me that my novel ORION had become a victim? He agreed that, of course, I had that right. When I asked him if, in telling my story, I uncovered questions regarding the death of Elvis and a possible cover-up, even possible hoaxing of his death, could I ask those questions?

Hugh, as part of the media, is trained to be a fair thinker. Yet I was not convinced he felt I had a legitimate right to questions regarding the possible cover-up in the death of Elvis Presley. I mentioned the 20/20 investigation. I also mentioned the KCOP TV news show which featured a picture possibly taken of Elvis *after* 1977, and I quoted that they asked about Elvis being alive. Hugh could not comment because he never saw that show. I mentioned a mystery tape which I had voice printed and which may have been recorded after 1977—a tape where Elvis discusses why he did what he did. Hugh said he knew nothing of that, either.

Although our conversation ended on a nice note, I felt drained and sad. Old doubts surfaced, making me unsure of my right to question.

Then I remember ORION.

The purpose of this book is not to exploit. It's to ask questions—mine and others. I'm not the only one in the media to ask or to speculate. I talked recently to Alana Nash, a journalist who was with the Louisville Courier at the time of Elvis' death. "I'm a logical person," she told me. "I went to the viewing, actually passed by the coffin twice. I've always felt it was a wax dummy. I thought then and still think that Elvis is alive."

Similar questions come from the fans, the backbone and foundation of the Presley financial empire. To discredit their right to these questions or to ridicule their beliefs is to shake that foundation.

Their questions are justified. I've outlined pages of legitimate mysteries—the misspelling of Elvis' name on his grave is enough. Still, there are times when I am thoroughly convinced there is a logical explanation for everything. At other times I am convinced Elvis is alive.

Under no circumstances would I have publically asked such questions had it not been for the disappearance of my novel ORION.

ORION did not deserve to be buried whether Elvis is or not.

"My Way"
—Elvis Presley Song—1973

A NEW LIFE

And there's more. Besides random telephone calls to disc jockeys, there were other calls, one to the co-presidents of THE ELVIS SPECIAL fan club. Because we can't see who is at the other end of the telephone line, what remains is guesswork. Finally, one is left with a mixture of clues and strange interviews, such as the one PLAYBOY did with singer John Denver, who stated he received a telegram from Elvis (and the Colonel) *after* Elvis died. Andy Kaufman, the comedian and co-star of television's TAXI made the statement, "Elvis is not dead." There's the incident when Maria Columbus, co-president of THE ELVIS SPECIAL, says she ran into Jerry Schilling, a friend of Elvis, at a local airport restaurant. He asked Maria to confirm the gossip about Elvis being alive, as reported in THE ELVIS SPECIAL. The name of Ellen Foster appears in various biographies, such as ELVIS AND GLADYS by Elaine Dundy. Essentially Ms. Foster says she met Elvis in early March of 1977. Ms. Foster looked so much like Elvis' mother, Gladys, that he thought the fan was a reincarnation of his mother. Elvis gave her a ring that belonged to his mother. Ms. Foster signed a sworn affidavit regarding her story. The ring is now on display. The obvious question as to its authenticity is why Ms. Foster waited until 1980 to present the ring to a museum. Vernon, the only one who could authenticate her story, had died the year before. However, it was not unknown or unusual for Elvis to give strangers gifts, and for a lot less reason than their looking like his mother. A similar story appears in a publication entitled ELVIS . . . WHERE ARE YOU? by Steven C. Chanzes. This time there is a reported interview with Ms. Foster concerning a telephone call she supposedly received from Elvis on August 14, 1977, the anniversary of his mother's death, and two days prior to his own "death." I tried to locate Ellen Foster, but my letter to her came back marked "returned to sender." I also attempted to locate the author of ELVIS . . . WHERE ARE YOU? but to no avail. Basically, Ms. Foster says Elvis telephoned her on the fourteenth and said he was not planning to go on the scheduled August 16th tour. She asked if he had cancelled it? He said he had not. She told him she did not understand, was he ill? He said he was fine, that she should not ask any more questions and that she should not tell anyone anything. When she said she did not understand what he was talking about he told her not to believe anything she read, that his troubles were all about to end, that he would eventually call her. He told her goodbye.

The author of ELVIS . . . WHERE ARE YOU? says that Ms. Foster took a polygraph test about this story and that she passed it.

In the book ARE YOU LONESOME TONIGHT?, Lucy de Barbin's story of the love she shared with Elvis and the birth of a daughter he never knew, she talks about Elvis calling her shortly before August 16, 1977. It was a conversation filled with Elvis planning to "clean" house, to begin a new life, and for Lucy to "trust him." Then came August 16th and the earth-shattering announcement: **Elvis Presley has died.**

Lucy described her disbelief and grief. Yet a few days after Elvis' "death" there was a knock at her door. She talked about a young man who handed her a single rose with a card from someone calling himself "El Lancelot" and pledging his love until he returned. "El Lancelot" was the code name Lucy said Elvis Presley used with her, as was the name "John Jones"—a name other biographies attest to.

ARE YOU LONESOME TONIGHT? has been the subject of controversy and, according to Geraldo Rivera on ENTERTAINMENT TONIGHT, is untrue. First, Lucy received a sentimental card from Elvis in 1973 which a handwriting expert has authenticated. Secondly, there is a Certificate of Live Birth listing the name of the father of Lucy's child as a "Randolph Presley."

Third, her daughter, Desiree, does look like Elvis Presley and fourth, Lucy is from Dallas, where she says she and Elvis met secretly over the years. In the many biographies I've studied, the remark is often repeated about Elvis having made sudden and unexplained trips to Dallas. Many of those around Elvis state they never heard of Lucy; others say her name was on the list of people to be put through to Elvis. Some say it would have been impossible for Elvis to go anywhere without their knowledge, which assumes each one of them was around Elvis twenty-four hours a day nonstop with no personal lives of their own. In addition we know that Elvis *did* slip away. On one occasion he slipped away to see the President of the United States! One newswriter speaks of several times when Elvis slipped away from Graceland and the Memphis Mafia to meet with him—once in the wee hours of the morning, another on the day before his death when they drove around the streets of Memphis with Elvis seeing the city of his home one last time.

Elvis was heard to have often remarked, "Everyone thinks they know what I'm thinking and what I'm doing . . . if they only knew."

As an aside, I also found it interesting that when the co-author of ARE YOU LONESOME TONIGHT?, Dary Matera, first met Desiree, it was at the Miami Airport where she was returning from a trip to South America. Recall the report from the Memphis Airport receptionist who says that on August 17, 1977 a man resembling Elvis Presley picked up a reserved ticket for Buenos Aires under the name of John Burrows?

Some questions concerning the death of Elvis are more intriguing than others. One concerns a picture snapped of Elvis driving into Graceland which shows him waving. "Since when were Elvis' fingers short and stubby?" questioned many fans via their newsletters.

Larry Blong, a dead-ringer for Elvis from Pennsylvania, revealed in a news interview how he was hired by Presley to dress like him and ride in a car in and out of Graceland waving to fans. This ruse gave Elvis an opportunity to come and go under another disguise. Known as "Double El," Larry recounts a time when he met Elvis at the gates where Elvis had ridden on a three-wheeler motorcycle. He stopped and called to Double El. "Hey, son, come here and listen to this." He had a recorder on the three-wheeler and started a cassette. At first Double El thought it was Elvis singing, but then realized it wasn't. When he asked Elvis who it was, Elvis laughed and shook his head.

I cannot help but wonder if this was the first time Elvis became aware of the existence of Jimmy Ellis, who would later become Orion. This recalls another late night telephone call from the voice. The call was timed with an appearance by the masked singer Orion at a country fair. I asked the voice if he was Orion? Hesitantly he said he wasn't, but then added, "The dude's good . . ."

I admitted I thought so too. "Do you know who Orion is?" I asked (I knew but I wanted to see if the caller did.)

The voice laughed shyly. "Well, I know who he's not."

I immediately called Carole Halupke and we once again tackled this growing enigma. "Maybe it's Elvis calling you," Carole reflected in disbelief. "What else makes sense?"

It was hard to make sense out of anything. Later I learned from disc jockey Doc Varb that Jimmy Ellis had been seen many times going in and out of Graceland. Playing upon this, perhaps since Elvis was known to use Double El for cover, could it be possible he was using Jimmy Ellis as a voice cover? After all, Ellis was used in the SUN RECORDS incident. Obviously, when the novel ORION came to SUN's attention, they used my book as a cover for the singer. Was it a double cover? Elvis loved masks, disguises, and the Captain Marvel, Jr./Lone Ranger logos. Was my attorney correct when he theorized that Orion could be a vocal cover for Elvis, that there were two voices on the albums, and that Elvis could perform via the mask without discovery? This certainly explains the sight of *two* Orions, *two* masked men. It also explains why on so many Orion albums the voice appears different, particularly with the Jerry Lee Lewis and Friends album.

Perhaps the novel ORION was originally meant to work as a convenient cover—no one would take its contents seriously if a masked singer of the same name appeared. It would look like a hoax or gimmick. But then along came the mass media's investigation into the death of Elvis Presley. Not long after both the novel and the singer disappeared. Telephone calls to SUN RECORDS did little to clarify why a singer with so much popularity and money behind him—expensive costumes, jewelry, bus and cars, would suddenly "drop out."

"Orion is no longer with us," was one reply.

"A contract disagreement," came another.

"He's singing under the name of Jimmy Ellis, not Orion," was a third explanation. "Legally he can't use the name Orion because we trademarked it."

The name Orion is a constellation and thus public domain. Moreso, SUN RECORDS did not simply use the name Orion—they used the name Orion E. Darnell. They used the Prologue of my novel on album covers as well as names and places copyrighted long before they took it upon themselves to trademark it. I checked with a copyright attorney, showed him the albums and promotional material, and he said it is a clear case of copyright infringement.

"You created a singer named Orion Darnell first, be it fiction or not," he explained. He cited some examples of character use from the novel GONE WITH THE WIND. "You have the protected right to authorize whomever you wish to be Orion Darnell." Since no legal agreements were drawn up with SUN, the entity known as Orion Darnell was mine to exploit via any means. I can hire or designate anyone, including Jimmy Ellis, to be Orion Darnell. In the novel, ORION, Orion Darnell is known by one name: Orion. As far as the mask, I was told that a precedent had already been set with the Lone Ranger issue. (The Lone Ranger was told he could not wear a mask, so he began wearing sunglasses until the issue was settled in court. From what I understand, a mask cannot be considered an exclusive in itself, no more than are wigs, jumpsuits, or capes.)

Thus, the reported reason as to Orion/Jimmy Ellis' disappearance makes no sense. SUN RECORDS is smart enough to know that the novel ORION came first and that they created their singer directly from the novel. So the only conclusion I can draw is that there are other reasons for the disappearance of Orion. Perhaps this book may help draw him out. He should not be penalized for having a voice comparable to the king.

I feel his talent, as well as my own, became secondary in a scheme. I believe we were both sacrificed without a great deal of thought. In the end it all comes around. Something *is* happening. I'm not the only person who feels this way.

In August of 1987 I received a telephone call regarding a 45 rpm record released by Prestige Productions in Birmingham, Alabama called DOWN IN MISSISSIPPI, sung by a singer named Steve Silver (Sivle? Silver also has the letters which form Elvis in it.) The voice on the record sounds like Elvis Presley. I wrote to the record distributor in Nashville and ordered some copies, which were amazingly inexpensive. I also spoke with Brenda Madden of DixiRaks Records & Tapes, the distributor. She said there was a mystery concerning the identity of Steven Silver, and that it was not the artist's real name. When I received the record I was intrigued by the lyrics as well as what might be two voices? Was this the Orion enigma all over again?

Basically the song is the story of Elvis Presley. He remembers Mississippi where the black folks picked cotton, dreaming of the day he could shake loose the Mississippi clay and become famous. There is a move to Memphis and a record cut for his mama overnight. A man called the Colonel signed him up and he became a king. Yet even though he becomes a star he never forgets his roots. One day he's no longer a kid with a Cadillac.

He's old. He's tired. He's a prisoner of his fame.

He prays. The Lord tells him he has to change his life.

But he was too famous. He had to change the way he looked. He went back to Mississippi, back to the simple ways.

He plays his guitar. No one knows him. Everyone thinks the king is gone. He's not. He's down in Mississippi where it's good to be back home.

The story is well-known. The song is not.

Apparently the songwriters think Elvis Presley may still be around.

DixiRaks
RECORDS & TAPES
1204 Elmwood Avenue
NASHVILLE, TENNESSEE 37212

1316

(615) 385-4282

Gail Brewer-Giorgio

DATE 8/24/87   JOB NO.

3809 Fox Hills Drive

JOB NAME

Marietta, GA 30067

JOB LOCATION

TERMS

		DESCRIPTION	PRICE	AMOUNT	
5	Vulcan-1060 - Steven Silver		@ 1.69	$	8	45
		Sub-Total		$	8	45
		Shipping		$	1	80
		Total		$	10	25
		Less Ck.#2634		$	10	25
		Total due		$	-	0-

ᴼ

ɹINAL

Thank You

The voice sounds like Elvis. Or is it Jimmy Ellis, Orion, or Silve? In the background, though, is another voice and it sounds a bit different. Obvious questions arise. There's no law against lyrics or a song that is a story, or even a tribute. Many have been done. It's obvious that the writers of this song, listed as Chance Jones, (Jones?) Mike Lantrip and Johnny Martin believe that Elvis may still be alive. And since the voice is so close to Elvis the record could cause some speculation. Yet the record has not been widely distributed. Also it sells for such a small amount of money that I find little financial gain to be made. When I called Prestige Productions, I spoke with Kenny Wallis, the producer of the record, and asked for some promotional material on the artist Steven Silver. I was told there wasn't any. I asked if Steven Silver would perform anywhere. I was told that was unlikely. Mr. Wallis admitted Steven Silver was not the true identity of the artist. To support this conversation, a woman named Renice Strain wrote to Mr. Wallis and received a letter which basically said, "Steven Silver is not the artist's real name. Because of an agreement with the artist and the company who does the promoting and distributing, we are not allowed to give the artist's real name . . ."

I asked Mr. Wallis if Steven Silver would record another record and he said he doubted it.

No laws have been broken. If the singer wishes to remain mysterious, that's his choice. From what I know of the music business, this is no way to gain fame or financial reward. And why, if it's Jimmy Ellis again, would he not reveal his name? Perhaps the record is an attempt to make the public believe it's Elvis and this is a message song. Again, this is strange if it is Jimmy Ellis, because as Orion, he made a point of saying he was not Elvis. My mind runs in circles playing out the various angles.

What I do know is there are at least three known names that lend themselves to mystery: Sivle, Orion, Silver. I have no idea if they are all the same voice or covers for another voice, or two voices. To continue to have each and every record voice printed is time-consuming and expensive. Each of these voices have one thing in common: they sound like Elvis Presley, and then the singer or singers mysteriously disappears.

Although Hugh Jarrett emphatically stated, "It *was* Elvis in the coffin," the people I've talked to who went to the viewing all say it did not look like Elvis, but more like a wax dummy. (Hugh did not go to the viewing.) The fan newsletters say it was not Elvis and members of Elvis' family report how "frighteningly different" Elvis looked in the coffin. In THE ELVIS SPECIAL there is a quote from country singer LaCosta (Tanya Tucker's sister): *"We went right up to his casket and stood there, and God, I couldn't believe it. He looked just like a piece of plastic laying' there. It didn't look like him at all . . . he looked more like a dummy than a real person. You know a lot of people think it WAS a dummy. They don't think he's dead."*

Please bear with me as I once again stress a point earlier made. Carole Halupke and I were at Mae Axton's when one of Elvis's songwriter-friends told us Vernon had admitted to him that it was not Elvis in the coffin and that Elvis was "upstairs."

If the wax dummy theory is true that explains the theory that the coffin weighed over 900 pounds; some believe it had an air conditioning unit built into it. Other people who managed to get close to the coffin report the air around the coffin was particularly cool. Recall that Larry Geller stated that one of Elvis' sideburns came loose, and he had to glue it back down, despite the fact Elvis had long sideburns the day before. People who knew Vernon thought it odd that if Elvis were dead, he would have put his son's body on display within an atmosphere resembling a circus. Alana Nash, the reporter from the Louisville Courier, agreed that this viewing was more of a "thou protest too much" type of response, an overreaction which stated: "See. He is dead. You can leave him alone. There's his body. See for yourself. He's gone."

Elvis and Vernon were upset when Gladys' funeral turned into a circus. I find it hard to believe that Vernon would have allowed such a repeat. "I think if it was the real thing," a fan told me, "it would have been a dignified and quiet ceremony. Instead it was a carnival."

This viewpoint is embraced by thousands of Elvis fans.

"And further," many state, "the fans were told we had plenty of time to get to Memphis for the viewing. We were never told it would be held in less than 24 hours. Many of us

172

think it was held quickly for a number of reasons, one being that the Colonel wanted the body out of the way quickly before questions arose about the cause of death, and the fact that everything disappeared, such as autopsy remains, reports and the like. And second, both Vernon and the Colonel knew that if the real fans had time to get to Memphis, we would have known it was not Elvis in the casket. How we were deceived has been the topic of most of our conversations, both at meetings and conventions. We do not believe Elvis ever died. We love him though, and we do understand. But that's what love's about, isn't it.'' A pause. ''I just hope no one goes after you for putting our questions and findings together in a book. If they do, I guess they'll have to go after us too. And our numbers are legion . . .''

''Someone already went after me,'' I whispered. ''And ORION, as well as myself, were its victim.''

I take the fans and their questions seriously. After all, they made a good judgment when they canonized Elvis Presley. Why should their judgments be any less valued now?

Before I get to the mystery tape and video, I am going to list some more questions the fans have. Some are repeats or extensions of material in the book, but they also stand alone:

Why did Elvis underscore in one of his spiritualistic books the following: ''Should I return, you would not recognize me.''?

Why did toward the end Elvis say ''Adios,'' when he had never done that before?

Why did Sonny West (one of the authors of ELVIS: WHAT HAPPENED? say at a press conference after Elvis' ''death'', that ''Elvis, wherever he was, knew he was telling the truth.''?

Why did Elvis turn to his stepbrother during his last concert tour just weeks before his ''death,'' and say, *''Know what, Rick? I may not look good for my television special tonight, but I'll look good in my coffin.''*?

And why during that final tour did he look down, his eyes away from the audience, fiddle with his fingers and then say, "I am, and I was"? and then quickly recover from his confession by bumping into the mike stand and attempting to laugh it off?

Was Elvis singing BLUE CHRISTMAS during his last concert tour a way of telling his fans that the coming Christmas would be without them? (Elvis' tour was a summer one and thus this song seemed out of place and out of season.)

Why was one of the titles of Elvis' last studio sessions the cut of THE LAST FAREWELL?

Did the song DANNY BOY, recorded at Elvis' home offer special meaning by stressing the lyrics: "As dead I well may be, yet he'll hear the footsteps of those treading above him."

Why was the song MY WAY launched toward the end? And, why, when Elvis knew its lyrics so well did he during his last concert, deliberately stop and read each word? (T.G. Sheppard is recorded as having noted how amazing Elvis' memory was.)

(Rick Stanley also reports that although Elvis liked the song MY WAY, he never made it a part of his show until the last year.)

Why did Elvis consent to having his last tour televised, knowing he was overweight and in ill health. Was it because August 16th was only weeks away and the money was needed?

Were the lyrics in the Moody Blue albums a clue to perhaps a plan to go out of the country, to South America? —"Way down" and "lonely rivers flow to the sea," and "I'll be coming home, wait for me."

Why were so many long-time employees released from their duties?

Why were all family members, despite Elvis' promises to the contrary, suddenly cut out of his will?

174

What happened to all of Elvis' savings accounts?

Was there insurance collected? Reportedly none. Why not?

Why did Rick Stanley reportedly comment that although Elvis remained thankful for life, death was more on his mind than living?

Why did Elvis in a reported last conversation with the singer Wayne Newton say, "Go on. Just remember, it's yours now. It's all yours . . ." (In an interview I read, Wayne Newton is said to have felt Elvis "knew he was going to die and that his choice of songs at the end were his way of saying goodbye to the world . . . every song was his Swan Song.")

Why did Rick Stanley say, after admitting he had stayed with Elvis until five or six that morning, that he had a prescription of Dilaudid filled, but it was in no way an amount that could have killed him? (Rick and other members of the family question the heart problem. Family members have also stated that questions about Elvis won't stop. People continue to say, "We know Elvis isn't dead. Where is he?" It has also been reported in one of the fan periodicals a stepbrother made this comment: "If Elvis is not dead and he did this, I'll never forgive him!")

Why did a woman who worked for Elvis at Graceland for nine years say in an interview, "I find it hard to believe that he died. There are just too many things that don't seem right. I wish they would dig up that casket and find out what's in it. He used to tell me that he was fed up with everything. 'Daisy,' he said, 'I wish I could go off and live by myself and not tell anybody where I am. Maybe on an island somewhere far away.' " (D.M. Williams in an interview with THE GLOBE.)

Why did Elvis suddenly begin wearing a "Chai" around his neck—especially since a Chai means a long and healthy life? Was this another clue?

Why is it rumored that Lloyds of London gave Elvis a clean bill of health shortly prior to August 16th.

What about the inventory of the estate? What about all the items not listed? Where are they? (On the copy I have, it lists only six pieces of jewelry. Elvis was known to have an extensive jewelry collection.)

Why were such personal items as photos, diaries, favorite books, missing from Elvis' room and the Inventory of the Estate?

According to a report in THE ELVIS SPECIAL, along with correspondence, one of those six pieces of jewelry, Elvis' famous TCB ring, has become controversial. Graceland reports in a letter to Maria Columbus, that Elvis had one of the TCB rings made for J.D. Summer which "is now on display in Pigeon Forge, Tennessee. The second ring (the one Elvis wore) is on display in the Trophy Room."

The question of why there was a TCB ring auctioned off in Beverly Hills in February of 1985 when only two were made was raised. "This leaves a lot of questions," asks Maria. "Is the ring on display at Graceland a fake? Or did Elvis have several identical TCB rings for himself? Did Elvis have a duplicate of the original made to use just at concerts? And who sold it? If there were two rings (owned by Elvis), why wasn't it reported in the Inventory of the Estate? If this wasn't Elvis' ring, why was it advertised using his name? Will we ever find out the facts?"

There is no end to the questions. Then comes the will: During a break from his grueling tour schedule for 1977, he took time out for a vacation trip to Hawaii. Before leaving, he decided to have a new will made. On March 3, 1977, a little over five months before his "death," he had a new will made. The will named Vernon Presley as executor of the estate. The will directed that a trust fund be established for Lisa Marie Presley. Upon the deaths of Minnie Mae (his grandmother) and Vernon, the estate was to be turned over to Lisa at the age of twenty-five. (When both Vernon and Minnie Mae died, Priscilla became executor.) The will gave Vernon absolute control of the estate and also gave Vernon "complete freedom and discretion as to any disposal of any and all such property as long as he shall act in good faith and in the best interest of my estate." The will excluded all friends, all charitable organizations, all longtime employees, and all family members except those mentioned.

Dee Presley has lamented in her book that Elvis had promised to take care of her boys, that they had given their lives to him, that in the end there was nothing. Why? Many of Elvis' longtime associates thought they would be "taken care of." The fans question how some of Elvis' closest friends appear to be living well despite no apparent income? In their assumptions that Elvis is alive, they wonder if he is providing for his friends, or if they are still working for him in some capacity?

Although I have repeatedly tried to remain objective, to present as complete and fair a picture as possible concerning what happened to me and to my novel ORION, along with letters, documentation, and interviews, there are many voids, many unanswered questions. Perhaps part of the answer lies in the question itself:

Is Elvis Presley alive?

Two important pieces of evidence that present the possibility of Elvis Presley being alive deserve attention. Both have been mentioned earlier. One is a video tape of a segment aired on Los Angeles KCOP's January 8, 1986 ten o'clock P.M. news. It features a story and a possible picture of Elvis Presley taken four months after his "death." The second is a taped conversation(s) supposedly around 1981.

Because I think the contents of both are important for evaluation, I am transcribing them in their entirety. My regret is that you, the reader, cannot personally view the picture as shown on the KCOP program.

As for the mystery tape: the results from a voice print expert were returned on December 15, 1987. Although the quality of the mystery tape is poor, it appears it is Elvis Presley. The Voice Identification Report as well as an analysis will follow the transcription.

Not long before he "died," he said, "The image is one thing, the human being another. It's very hard to live up to an image." Toward the end many heard him say, "I feel intensely lonely at heart."

"And now the end is near," he both read and sang before the Grand Finale. "I'll do it my way . . ."

Perhaps in the end he did.

KCOP Television, Los Angeles—10 o'clock, P.M. News— January 8, 1986

Tim Malloy co-anchor with Wendy Rutledge. The title of the news segment: LONG LIVE THE KING. The transcript begins with Tim Malloy, speaking:

"Well, now here's a story about Elvis that probably belongs in the twi-light zone or more appropriately the night gallery, because it is about a picture, a picture taken after the king's death, one that has made people wonder if Elvis has left this world, or at all? Bob Walsh has more on this mysterious story:"

(Bob Walsh's voice)

"Mike Joseph took his family to Graceland for a vacation on January 1st of 1978, more than four months after the death of Elvis Presley—perhaps we should say 'reported death.' At the time the grounds of Graceland were the only part of the estate open to the public, but Joseph took some snapshots and put them away for safe-keeping. Four years later while reading about Presley, Joseph took out his mementos of the Graceland visit, and he noticed something unusual in a shot of the bathhouse behind the mansion. It was a shadow in the lower half of the door. Joseph says he had the pictures enlarged and the results were nothing short of startling. Someone or something bearing a remarkable resemblance to Elvis Presley was indeed sitting behind the door. Playboy Magazine bought the temporary rights to the pictures for an undisclosed amount of money but never published them. Joseph says Playboy and other publications who bid on the pictures weren't sure of just exactly how to handle the story."

178

(Mike Joseph now speaks)

"They thought it was the most amazing photograph they've ever seen. Everybody, ah, they didn't know what to think— how to present it—I just told them just present it as a photograph that was taken four months after he died."

(Back to Bob Walsh)

"The picture in question is part of a set. All the negatives are intact, and a spokesman for Playboy confirms that the pictures were not doctored. The sequence of pictures including shots of Elvis' grave confirms that the pictures were indeed taken after Presley's death. Joseph says he's not trying to convince anyone that Elvis still lives or that the snapshot is an image of some supernatural phenomenon but there is something there. How it got there and what it is will no doubt remain as much a mystery as the entire Presley mystique."*

The mystery tape was presented to me in front of several witnesses: MaryBeth Danielski, Tom and Carolyn Brewer.

The two women who came to my home refused to tell me their identity, but the one did say she was married to a member of the Presley family. The tape was presented as Elvis, although it was made clear to me that the tape had been altered, meaning that whoever Elvis was talking to cut their voice out. I was told to get a voice print done, that it would prove their story. They contacted me because they knew what had happened to the novel ORION and they believed the novel was stopped because I had come too close to the truth. They spent several hours here and although cautious, they began to open up. After the women left, a discussion was held and notes matched. The end result was I believed there was enough to their story to have a voice print done.

*I, along with countless others, have viewed this picture. If it is Elvis, his face is full, which makes sense since it was taken only four months after his "death," and he may not have lost a great deal of weight. The fact that someone is looking out the door is quite clear. I can make out eyeglasses, non-tinted or slightly tinted. I can see his eyes. It is a remarkable picture and surely justifies the questions asked by the fans, by the media at large, and by me.

I contacted voice print expert L. H. Williams of Houston, Texas. He took a known voice of Elvis Presley and through analysis indicated in his conclusion that the unknown speaker (mystery tape) and known speaker (Elvis Presley) are the same.

However, I want to make it clear that I have no idea when this recording (supposedly over the telephone) was made. Mr. Williams also stated that the entire cassette was not made at one sitting and was instead the result of more than one recording. This could have been done in many ways:

1. If Elvis had telephoned someone on various occasions and unknowingly been recorded, that person may have put the majority of the recordings on one cassette, deliberately leaving their voice and identity off.
2. (I was told the reason the person Elvis is supposedly talking to wants their identity unknown is for fear of being involved in a death hoax.)
3. The tape could have been spliced together by taking dialogue from various films and creating a story whereby people think he's hoaxed his death.
4. It is a splicing from other interviews.

I've thought each possibility out. But when I listen to the tape and read the dialogue there are too many instances when "Elvis" refers to being in hiding, growing a beard, to having friends fear he will be found out. I have chosen to include the tape transcription here, as well as the Voice Identification Report.

You be the judge.

Mystery Tape (Believed to have been recorded around 1981) Transcription:

People ask me all the time where I'm living, and actually I can't say but uh, it's a good place to hide. I, uh, it actually started when I arrived in Hawaii. I made uh, I made arrangements with a friend of mine to uh fly me out of the state. You know it was uh, it was really something because everything worked just like it was meant to be. I mean uh, there was an island I had learned about a long time ago and uh I guess I always knew some day I'd probably have to use it anyway. I must have spent a year on the island. I really can't say that I didn' need the rest. Slowly, I started getting myself in shape. I didn't sing much. I'd needed the rest even more than I knew. But after about a year I started missing the people and entertaining. I mean I've been entertaining people the better part of my life and it's very hard to stop doing something that you've been doing that long.

But I uh, I started traveling all over the world and it's been uh, it's been enjoyable but it's been a constant battle of growing beard and this and that to keep from being recognized and I guess, I guess about two years ago I went to Europe which is something I've always wanted to do for a long time. I mean I've always been sorry that I didn't go to Europe before but I could have, I guess I just didn't uh, I just didn't take the time.

Anyway, uh, the first place that I wanted to see in Germany was a place called Weisbaden. I don't know whether or not you've ever seen Weisbaden before but uh, my girlfriend was with me and we went to a place just to get something to eat and uh, a waitress there asked me what we liked to have and I said, I don't know really I—what would you suggest and she stood still. She kept staring at me and uh, I started getting very nervous. At the time I had a beard and I lost a few pounds and I thought it would be, I thought it would be very hard for anyone to recognize me. Then uh, she asked me if I've ever been in Germany in the past, and then I got more nervous, but uh, she said I, I never forget a face and then she said, I don't know how you did it, but she said, I don't care how you did it. She said I just hope that your as happy as you made me tonight.

And you know that's, that's the type experience that I'll never forget.

There's been uh, there's been a lot of times, I, I would like to have changed some things, but I've learned that when something is done you, you can't look back. I mean sometimes it's not good to look back.

I, I think you know that, that she, she means as much to me as life itself. And hopefully the good Lord willing, sometime fate will be kind to us, and, and I'll see her again.

As far as enjoying life now, you know I, I could go to

football games and to the movies but what interests me most is seeing people in a way that, that I hadn't before. I mean I've talked to people that have been sick and, and I, I thought I could help in some way. And for me that has to be the best part of life.

As far as, as far as she is concerned or, or any part of my family I, I really don't think it's a good idea right now. I mean there's, there's no hard feelings or anything but shes, shes always wanted her own life, and it makes me happy just to see that she's all right. You know uh, a lot of times people walk up to me and they say that uh, their concerned about, about people, about people finding out and then they think about it for a while, and, and then they usually say that nobody would believe them anyway.

I, I, I don't know. In, in the first place it would be, it would be foolish to walk back into a life style that, that I just escaped from but I'm going to continue my music and give people as much of what they want as I can. I've had a, I've had people write letters to me that I've been just fantastic. It's, it's nice to know that there are people that are truly concerned about you that much. I mean you have to do something and there's, there's a lot of things I would like to do and, and there's a lot of music that I would like to attempt.

As far as, as my dating is concerned uh, uh, (laugh) I, I still date. I'm dating a young lady right now that, that has been very helpful to me, as far as keeping my sanity, and she's been good for me. When we uh, when we first met she kept telling me how much she liked my music. She, she kind of looked at me in shock when we first met, like most people, but, she was glad I was still here and you know one thing led to another and now she, she goes with me just about every place I go. I mean uh, it's, it's nice. I, I have a lot, a lot of time on my hands now, and I'm getting, I'm getting back into sports a lot, and I'm still working out and playing racketball and karate whenever I get a chance. It's, it's helped me to, to stay in shape and, and the clean living surely can't hurt.

You know that's, that's one that has always gotten to me. I mean there's a lot of people that are making a lot of money off the drug thing and if that's what makes them happy, that's fine. But it's not true. The fact of the matter is that I haven't

182

even taken a sleeping pill in three years. If I had the uh, if I had the chance to do everything again I'd probably make the same mistakes but uh, if you, you grow attached to people who are with you and your life a lotta times becomes more important to people than, than you can realize yourself sometimes. You know that's uh, you try to help as many people as you can and, and sometimes, sometimes you try to please someone and sometimes you can't please anybody.

No, a lot of times I, I felt the image hurt me but uh, I always knew there'd be a price I'd have to pay. You know there's, there's a lot of people that are lonely. I mean you don't have to be on the poor side of life to be lonely. You don't have to be rich to be lonely. You can be standing in a group of a hundred people and be lonely.

Strange thing, you know, :um, lately, I, I've been trying to write music which is something I, I always wanted to do and I just never took the time and, and I'm trying to play the guitar better. I still play the piano.

I've spent most of my time getting myself back into shape. It's not easy to get everything done at the same time. There's been uh, there's been a lot of things that have happened. I've got to be, I've got to be very careful. I mean uh, I met a young lady in a supermarket once and she kept following me. Finally she said, "I almost can't believe, but uh, I think I know who you are", and I said, "uh, honey, if you don't tell anybody, I said I won't", and right then and there in the supermarket she started crying and I said, "honey don't you cry", and the tears just started falling down her face and she put her arms around me and she said, "I feel I know what you been through", she said, "I'll always love you", and you know things like that are, are experiences that you just can't, a you can't buy.

It's very hard. It's very hard to forget anything like that, but uh, things like that have uh, have been happening to me uh, a lot.

I don't think uh, I don't think anybody can tell really what's going to happen one day to the next. Uh, I'm not completely hiding now you know. I mean I'm seen by people all the time. As far as appearing nationally I think it would be silly to say the least, to be back into something that's taken me this long to get out of. But uh, I'd like to do, I'd like to

183

continue my music. I'd like to do some new things. I'd like to do some things that uh, because of contracts or something couldn't be done in the past. But uh, mostly I just want to, I want to continue to entertain people I've said it before and uh, it's something that's in my mind and uh, I just would like to get into it not as much as I used to and I'm sure that uh, sometime in the near future I, it has to happen, but until it does I'll just go on living as normal life as I possibly can.

I've been uh, I've been very lucky. I also believe that as I said the Lord has been on my side. Sometimes I feel like instead of being an Island, or on an Island, I am an Island. You know it uh, it's kinda, it's kinda hard to go through this life just, just memories and it seems like that's what I have now, but I would still like to give back a lot to people that have been so much to me.

I'm a, I'm hoping that, that a lot of people out there are not disappointed with me. I mean I didn't mean to put anybody through any pain . . . It uh, it's taken a lot to uh, have to do what I had to do. But uh, I think in the long run it's going to pay off. I believe that in doing things like this may have made it a lot easier for me and for everybody else.

I don't know, it's, life is very strange. I, I have gone through so many different types of experiences that I don't even, I don't even know sometimes where I'm at, but I've learned a lot, the things I've gone through. I'm always learning more. There isn't anyway you can stop learning, you have to continue to learn.

I know there's a lot of movies that, that have come out in the past and uh, the recent past that uh, I haven't enjoyed at all. It's, it's interesting that when you're involved in entertaining you realize that, that there's a lot of things like an image, and various other things that people try to portray. They try to make you a certain way and uh, I think they done the same thing with the movies. You know they want to make things come out a certain way and if they don't, you know, I guess they feel they haven't done their job. But uh, just like the drug thing now that I was talking about, movies, a lot of it was just simply not true. There isn't a lot that I can do about it you know, I wish that uh, I wish they'd ask me about it before they made the movie, but there isn't a lot that I can do right now.

I do believe that there were a lot of people that never forget and that's good because sometimes you feel as though your the only one with any memories and uh, it's nice to feel that people, they remember too.

I'm looking forward to spending this coming Christmas in a new way. It's always been a very happy time of the year for me and uh, I'm looking forward to it. I'm looking forward to uh, possibly seeing some people that, that are going to be shocked. I, I'm just hoping that these people that I'm goin to see won't be hurt, but I know there going to be shocked. It's gonna be good and because Christmas time is, is a good time of year to make everything okay, to amend. And so if there's ever a time I could make an appearance or that I could come out into the open, I think, uh, I think Christmas time would be it.

I'm looking forward to a lot of good things in the future. I made a lot of good friends and I just think that uh, I think it's gonna be better this time. I could look out the window now and I can see a lot. I can see a lot more then I ever have and I guess the reason for that is because I, I can actually go the place I'm looking at and I can be alone. I can be around people and do the type of the things I like to do without havin a hundred people there by my side you know, it's a different experience for me, it's a good experience.

I realize that sooner or later it's probably gonna end. You know I hate to think it's gonna end but I know sometime the secret is got to be let out and if and if it hadn't been for getting involved in what I'm involved in now you know, things or such, maybe it'd be different, but it's not and uh, I have to do my music. There's no getting around it. I just can't go on without entertaining. So, so hopefully things will work out better this time. I don't know, just have to wait and see. I know that I've been very fortunate as I said and the Lord has helped me through everything and I don't see how this can be any different.

I think there's new things coming and uh, it's gonna be good for everybody. I would like to, I'd like to finish the book that's been already started about my life as far as what I have been doing in the past three to four years. I'm working on an album. Something I wanted to do in the last few years were trying to get hold of some people who have helped me in the past, you know to help me with the music and put out maybe the best album I've ever put out. I don't know if uh, I, we can get hold of all the people but we're working on it and it's something everyone can look forward to.

I think uh, a lot of people have given me the chance to continue without bringing me too far into the open. It's taken a lot to get me uh, in hiding and it would be uh, a shame if things just turn around in five seconds but uh, it's given me a lot of time to work whereas before I, I didn't have any time to work. I just constantly had to do the same things over and over again as far as music is concerned and I kept putting out the same things all the time.

It's hard to get something the way you want it and to change it drastically if you've been, if you've been used to the way you've been doing it in the past and especially if you haven't, if you haven't got any time. I, I didn't have any time before. My time was taken up, but this is different. This gives me a chance to, to really get into something to make it a piece of material that uh, I can do the way I want to do it instead of, instead of the way somebody else telling me they want some way and, and this and that and just makin it a big uh, mess. You know I just have to, I just have to do things this time the way I want it and I, I think it will work a lot better.

The first album that we already released is something that uh, was done a few months ago and uh, I enjoyed it but I, I'll tell you I didn't really think we would ever release it. I, I was remembering all my songs and things and it was a lot of fun you know. I had a lot of fun doin it, but uh, the next album that we put out I really hope that we can get hold of everyone that's helped in the past because I, it's gonna be a, it would be a rewarding experience to think that uh, that every thing could work so smoothly.

I, my whole life has been something out of a dream, to have this happen, I mean to, to get all the people together that helped me in the past to, to help with the new album and uh, help me with me with everything that already has happened, it would uh, it would have to be the biggest experience in my life and I'm certain it would be good for them too. I'm looking forward to it and you know many times we, we despair and we think that, that life has somehow passed us by, but you know dreams can come true.

186

December 15, 1987

VOICE IDENTIFICATION REPORT

EVIDENCE
SUBMITTED:

One (1) C-60 audio cassette purported to contain the voice of Elvis Presley from Gail Brewer-Giorgio. One (1) C-60 audio cassette containing the known voice of Elvis Presley taken during an interview on a motion picture set in 1962.

ANALYSIS
REQUIERD:

Both aural and spectrographic in an attempt to determine (a) whether the voice in question is indeed that of Elvis Presley and / or (b) any other discernible factors involved in the production of this audio tape.

METHOD:

A. Accepted procedures of aural and spectrographic analysis comparing the purported voice of Elvis Presley against that of a known sample.
B. Such methods as were applicable and available as referred to in The Authentication of Magnetic Tapes: Current Problems and Possible Solutions by Weiss and Hecker.

PROBLEMS
INCURRED
AND SOLUTIONS
ATTEMPTED:

A.   Voice Identification was random text versus random text. The quality of the unknown voice was good but did contain low vocal volume with a high ambient noise level.   As an attempted solution to these problems, the vocal volume was raised to an acceptable level while the high ambient noise level was filtered to achieve the clearest possible audio level possible.   Voice Identification utilized the comparison of thirty-five (35) various mono and multi

VOICE IDENTIFICATION REPORT CONTINUED:

syllabic words and / or phrases.

B. As stated in A. above, the overall volume of speechsound in the unknown was low and somewhat covered by ambient noise. The raising of the volume level and filtering of those frequencies which lie above the normal speech range (those above 4000 Hz) brought the needed information to a workable level.

CONCLUSIONS: A. After comparing thirty-five (35) unknown words of random text against thirty-five (35) known words of random text and considering the possible variables of multiple recordings, tape speeds, and the various types of recording equipment involved, I have concluded that there is data indicating that the unknown and known speakers are the same with a moderate level of confidence.

B. After enhancing the tape in question and numerous aural and spectrographic examinations, I have determined that their are several start/stops, audio dropouts, and more than one recording method applied to the unknown audio tape in question based upon information from the above named paper.

REMARKS:

Although the full Voice Identification process as prescribed by the International Association for Identification, Voice Identification and Acoustic Analysis was not possible due to the constraints in this particular instance, I feel that a minimal decision is warranted and thus reached my decision within the time and quality constraints which were present.

Tape authentication per se cannont be completed with this particular tape due to its origin as the original tapes would be necessary. I do not know whether the

VOICE IDENTIFICATION REPORT CONTINUED:

edited and re-recorded portions are accidental or
intentional. They obviously do exist just as the
indication that the first half of the audio portion was
recorded in a different manner or from a different
source than the last half. The whispered "that" which
is perceived toward the end of the tape is of unknown
origin.

L. H. Williams
Voice Identification and
Acoustic Analysis

4/15/88

BACKGROUND: Legend Books approached me with one C-62 cassette
tape. I was told that the tape contained the
voice of Elvis Presley and had been voice printed
for authenticity. I was asked to record and edit
an interview with Gail Brewer-Giorgio and Jeff Prugh
and insert portions of the Presley tape between
interview segments. I also was asked to filter
the Presley tape to improve audibility and remove
as much background noise and hiss as possible.
I only performed two edits on the Presley tape.
In each case no program material was removed, only
10 to 15 seconds of silence. It should also be
noted that the provided tape was not the original
recording and that the person or persons Presley was
talking to have very crudely removed their voices
from the tape prior to my recieving it.

OPINION: It is my opinion that this tape was not pieced
together, word by word, from other interviews.
Furthermore, large sections (3 to 4 minutes)
show no signs of any editing whatsoever. Basicly,
the speaker spoke these sentences and groups of
sentences and this tape is not a product of words from
many interviews being put together. I base this
opinion on over ten years of editing voice tapes
as well as supporting conversations with other tape
editors. The specific points supporting my
conclusion are; voice stress, recording quality,
absence of tell-tale edits, and the background
noise.

Voice Stress: Voice stress and level are consistant
in each sentence. If words are added or taken out
of an existing tape it is impossible to achieve an
even voice stress between words, especially if words
are lifted from seperate interviews. The voice stress
and speech patterns flow in this tape, they do not
chop and it is this flow that an editor can not create.

Recording Quality: Recording quality and level are
consistant within the sentences which means that all
the words would have had to come from a single
interview or interviews conducted under the same
conditions.

Absence of Tell-tale Edits: There are no signs of editing within the sentences or between the sentences of any given topic. Such signs would be truncated words or unnatural word patterns. Studders and slured words which abound in this tape are particularly difficult to edit well enough so that they are undetectable.

Background Noise: The background noise on this tape is consistant and flows thru and between sentences. While it is possible that a clever editor could use this noise to masque very small problems with his edits, the noise would not be able to cover up changes in voice stress or recording conditions. If, as I believe, the noise is on the original tape and was a product of poor recording technique, (perhaps a suction cup microphone on a telephone), then the noise by itself is proof that no editing was done within sentences or topics.

CONCLUSION: The tape of Elvis Presley that Legend Books is distributing is not a product of one or more interviews being edited together, word by word, Simply, these sentences were spoken as sentences, and if the voice print is true, then these were sentences and topics spoken in their entirety by Elvis Presley.

Don Moran
Audio Engineer/Operations Mgr.
L.T.L. Enterprises, Inc.

The Attached documentation can be obtained from:

Freedom of Information Act Request
Chief, Disclosure Branch
Office of Assistant to the Director
(Public Affairs and Disclosure)
Bureau of Alcohol, Tobacco and Firearms
Room 4405 FE
1200 Pennsylvania Avenue, N.W.
Washington, D.C. 20226

According to press reports following the meeting between Elvis Presley and President Richard Nixon, in order for Elvis Presley to be presented an official narcotic badge he was made a special "consultant" with credentials for the Bureau of Narcotics and Dangerous Drugs.

Note that on File Number 822255 Elvis Presley provided an undercover agent of the government with a job cover. On File Number 822314, the government cannot elaborate on the investigative role this agent played, although it is clear Elvis was aware that an investigation of "something" was taking place. It is unclear as to what Elvis Presley's role was in all of this.

Note also on the handwritten letter to President Nixon from Elvis Presley that his code name was indeed "Jon Burrows."

MEMORANDUM

THE WHITE HOUSE

WASHINGTON

December 21, 1970

MEMORANDUM FOR: MR. H. R. HALDEMAN

FROM: DWIGHT L. CHAPIN

SUBJECT: Elvis Presley

Attached you will find a letter to the President from Elvis Presley.
As you are aware, Presley showed up here this morning and has
requested an appointment with the President. He states that he knows
the President is very busy, but he would just like to say hello and
present the President with a gift.

As you are well aware, Presley was voted one of the ten outstanding
young men for next year and this was based upon his work in the
field of drugs. The thrust of Presley's letter is that he wants to become
a "Federal agent at large" to work against the drug problem by com-
municating with people of all ages. He says that he is not a member
of the establishment and that drug culture types, the hippie elements,
the SDS, and the Black Panthers are people with whom he can communicate since he is not part of the establishment.

I suggest that we do the following:

 This morning Bud Krogh will have Mr. Presley in and talk
 to him about drugs and about what Presley can do. Bud will
 also check to see if there is some kind of an honorary agent
 at large or credential of some sort that we can provide
 for Presley. After Bud has met with Presley, it is recommended that we have Bud bring Presley in during the Open
 Hour to meet briefly with the President. You know that
 several people have mentioned over the past few months that
 Presley is very pro the President. He wants to keep everything
 private and I think we should honor his request.

I have talked to Bud Korgh about this whole matter, and we both think
that it would be wrong to push Presley off on the Vice President since
it will take very little of the President's time and it can be extremely
beneficial for the President to build some rapport with Presley.

In addition, if the President wants to meet with some bright young
people outside of the Government, Presley might be a perfect one to
start with.

You
be

Approve Presley coming in at end of Open Hour ___*H.*___

Disapprove_____

Dear Mr. President.

First I would like to introduce myself. I am Elvis Presley and admire you and Have Great Respect for your office. I talked to Vice President Agnew in Palm Springs 3 weeks and expressed my concern for our country. The Drug Culture, The Hippie Elements, the SDS, Black Panthers, etc do not consider me as their enemy or as they call it the Establishment. I call it America and I Love it. Sir I can and Will be of any Service that I can to help The country out. I have no concern or motives other than helping the country out. So I wish not to be given a title or an appointed position. I can and will do more good if I were made a Federal agent at Large, and I will help best by doing it my way through my communication with people of all ages. First and Foremost I am an entertainer but all I need is the Federal credentials. I am on this Plane with

Sen. George Murphy and We
have been discussing the problems
that our Country is faced with.
So I am Staying at the Washington
hotel Room 505-506-507. I have
2 men who work with me by the
name of Jerry Schilling and Sonny
West. I am registered under the name
of Jon Burrows. I will be here
for as long as it takes to get
the credentials of a Federal Agt.
I have done an in depth study of
Drug abuse and Communist Brainwashing

Techniques and I am right in the
middle of the whole thing. Where
I can and will do the most good
I am Glad to help just so long
as it is kept very Private. You can
have your staff or whoever call
me anytime today tonight or Tomorrow
I was nominated the coming year
one of America's Ten most outstanding
young men. That will be in January
18 in my Home Town of Memphis Tenn.
I am sending you the short autobiography
about myself so you can better understand this

~~approach~~

approach. I would love to
meet you just to say hello if
you're not to Busy.
Respectfully
Elvis Presley

P.S. I believe that you Sir
were one of the Top Ten Outstanding Men
of America also.

I have a personal gift for you also
which I would like to present to you
and you can accept it or I will keep it
for you until you can take it

Mr. President NUMBERS

These numbers are PVT numbers	
Beverly Hills	278-3496
	278-5935
Palm Springs Pvt	325-3241
Memphis	397-4427
	298-4882
	398-9722
Pvt.	
Col. P.S.	325-4781
Col. R.H.	279-8498
Col. Off. mem	870-0870

WASHINGTON HOTEL) PHONE ME 85900
RM 505-506.
UNDER THE NAME
OF JON BURROWS

PRIVATE
AND CONFIDENTIAL

Atten. President Nixon
Via Sen George Murphy
from
Elvis Presley

THE WHITE HOUSE

WASHINGTON

December. 21, 1970

MEMORANDUM FOR: THE PRESIDENT'S FILE

SUBJECT: Meeting with Elvis Presley
                      Monday, December 21, 1970
                      12:30 p. m.

The meeting opened with pictures taken of the President and Elvis Presley.

Presley immediately began showing the President his law enforcement para-
phernalia including badges from police departments in California, Colorado
and Tennessee. Presley indicated that he had been playing Las Vegas and
the President indicated that he was aware of how difficult it is to perform
in Las Vegas.

The President mentioned that he thought Presley could reach young people,
and that it was important for Presley to retain his credibility. Presley responded that he did his thing by "just singing." He said that he could not
get to the kids if he made a speech on the stage, that he had to reach them
in his own way. The President nodded in agreement.

Presley indicated that he thought the Beatles had been a real force for anti-
American spirit. He said that the Beatles came to this country, made their
money, and then returned to England where they promoted an anti-American
theme. The President nodded in agreement and expressed some surprise.
The President then indicated that those who use drugs are also those in the
vanguard of anti-American protest. Violence, drug usage, dissent, protest
all seem to merge in generally the same group of young people.

Presley indicated to the President in a very emotional manner that he was
"on your side." Presley kept repeating that he wanted to be helpful, that
he wanted to restore some respect for the flag which was being lost. He
mentioned that he was just a poor boy from Tennessee who had gotten a lot
from his country, which in some way he wanted to repay. He also mentioned
that he is studying Communist brainwashing and the drug culture for over
ten years. He mentioned that he knew a lot about this and was accepted by
the hippies. He said he could go right into a group of young people or hippies
and be accepted which he felt could be helpful to him in his drug drive. The
President indicated again his concern that Presley retain his credibility.

At the conclusion of the meeting, Presley again told the President how much he supported him, and then, in a surprising, spontaneous gesture, put his left arm around the President and hugged him.

In going out, Presley asked the President if he would see his two associates. The President agreed and they came over and shook hands with the President briefly. At this meeting, the President thanked them for their efforts and again mentioned his concern for Presley's credibility.

Bud Krogh

THE WHITE HOUSE

WASHINGTON

December 21, 1970

A/

MEMORANDUM FOR: THE PRESIDENT

SUBJECT: Meeting with Elvis Presley
December 21, 1970
12:30 p. m.

I.   PURPOSE

To thank Elvis Presley for his offer to help in trying to stop
the drug epidemic in the country, and to ask him to work with
us in bringing a more positive attitude to young people throughout the country.

In his letter to you, Elvis Presley offered to help as much as
possible with the growing drug problem. He requested the
meeting with you this morning when he presented himself to
the guard at the Northwest Gate bearing a letter.

II.   PARTICIPANTS

Elvis Presley

Bud Krogh (staff)

III.   TALKING POINTS

A.   We have asked the entertainment industry - both television
and radio - to assist us in our drug fight.

B.   You are aware that the average American family has 4 radio
sets; 98% of the young people between 12 and 17 listen to
radio. Between the time a child is born and he leaves high
school, it is estimated he watches between 15,000 and
20,000 hours of television. That is more time than he spends
in the classroom.

C. The problem is critical: As of December 14, 1970, 1,022 people died this year in New York alone from just narcotic related deaths. 208 of these were teenagers.

D. Two of youth's folk heroes, Jimi Hendrix and Janis Joplin, recently died within a period of two weeks reportedly from drug-related causes. Their deaths are a sharp reminder of how the rock music culture has been linked to the drug sub-culture. If our youth are going to emulate the rock music stars, from now on let those stars affirm their conviction that true and lasting talent is the result of self motivation and discipline and not artificial chemical euphoria.

E. Suggestions for Presley activities:

 1. Work with White House Staff

 2. Cooperate with and encourage the creation of an hour Television Special in which Presley narrates as stars such as himself sing popular songs and interpret them for parents in order to show drug and other anti-establishment themes in rock music.

 3. Encourage fellow artists to develop a new rock musical theme, "Get High on Life."

 4. Record an album with the theme "Get High on Life" at the federal narcotic rehabilitation and research facility at Lexington, Kentucky.

 5. Be a consultant to the Advertising Council on how to communicate anti-drug messages to youth.

DEPARTMENT OF THE TREASURY
BUREAU OF ALCOHOL, TOBACCO AND FIREARMS
WASHINGTON, D.C. 20226

NOV 2 9 1982

OFFICE OF
THE DIRECTOR

REFER TO
822255

This is in response to your undated request for information
concerning the Certificate of Appreciation awarded to Elvis
Presley in 1976 by the Bureau of Alcohol, Tobacco and Firearms.

During the period of 1974 through 1976, Mr. Presley provided
one of our undercover agents, who was a musician, a job cover.
Mr. Presley confirmed to anyone inquiring that the agent/musician
was a member of one of his traveling bands. Although Mr. Presley
was not actively involved in any of the investigations, his
assistance in this regard made it possible for our agent to
develop a number of quality investigations. The certificate was
presented to Mr. Presley by the Regional Director of BATF,
Mr. William Griffin.

Mr. Presley's visit to the White House in 1970, was not related
to his assistance to this Bureau. Although I am not sure,
I believe that President Nixon recognized Mr. Presley's
contribution and assistance to the Drug Enforcement Agency.

Sincerely yours,

Bob Pritchett
Chief, Disclosure Branch

DEPARTMENT OF THE TREASURY
BUREAU OF ALCOHOL, TOBACCO AND FIREARMS
WASHINGTON, D.C. 20226

OFFICE OF
THE DIRECTOR

DEC 2 2 1982

REFER TO
822314

This is in response to your letter, dated December 7, 1982,
in which you asked for additional information about
Elvis Presley. There were no photographs taken; nor are
there any materials available that you could see.

We are unable to comment on any of the many rumors, and
obviously we cannot identify the agent involved, who is not
willing to elaborate on his undercover role. Most of the
files are Criminal Investigative files and do not mention
or involve Mr. Presley. The fact is Mr. Presley was not
aware of these investigations. All he knew was that our
agent needed a cover story.

I am sorry I cannot be of further assistance to you in
this matter.

Sincerely yours,

Bob Pritchett
Chief, Disclosure Branch

UPDATE 1988

What has happened since the release of the First Tele-arketing Edition of THE MOST INCREDIBLE ELVIS PRESLEY STORY EVER TOLD!, retitled for the paperback edition as IS ELVIS ALIVE? is interesting.

Daily, new information arrives that raises even more questions:

Several fans wrote questioning, why, after being offered the American Flag for his son's funeral, Vernon Presley turned it down. After all, Elvis was a veteran and his patriotism was applauded. "Is it because Elvis did not die," they questioned, "and Elvis would never commit patriotic fraud?" Or, on the other hand, if he had indeed died, "wouldn't Vernon Presley readily have accepted such a patriotic tribute to his only son?"

We tracked down the gentleman who worked with the IRS and who checked the books for the estate. Because of his position we cannot identify him. However he would appear in a court of law. We asked him if there were strange monetary transactions. He said yes. (None illegal though.) He also said that it was very strange that no insurance had been collected.

On a news program in 1979 NBC focused in on a twenty million dollar coal tax scheme involving two financial decisions made by Elvis Presley shortly before his death which were completely out of character. Elvis Presley was known to not be an investor and two, Elvis never tried to avoid paying taxes. Yet Elvis invested $500,000 in the coal industry, and although cheated out of his investment he did not suffer but instead was allowed to take advantage of a tax loophole which allowed investors to take income tax deductions of up to five times the amount invested, which meant a two-and-a-half million dollar tax advantage for Elvis.

Again, this was not illegal, only "out of character" for Elvis. And it gave him excess funds shortly pre August 16, 1977.

Not only was Elvis in ill health, but according to Ed Parker in his own book, INSIDE ELVIS, Elvis was constantly the target of assassination plots.

I had heard and read this countless times but upon meeting more and more of those who knew Elvis, I have learned of the daily fear he faced, not so much for himself but for members of his family, particularly Lisa. The pressure of being Elvis Presley was compounded minute by minute. Is it any wonder he told Felton Jarvis, his record producer, shortly before August 16th, "I am sick and tired of being Elvis Presley . . ."

As one rereads and rereads the man biographies done on Elvis by family and friends you are struck by incredible conversations. Another that has come to my attention occurred between Elvis' stepbrother David Stanley and Elvis only days before his "death."

David reports that Elvis had been in a very strange mood, a mood David is unable to get out of his mind. Apparently David was about to leave and Elvis began to cry and then hugged him, telling him how much he loved David. David responded in like and then Elvis told him he would never see him again, at least not on this plane.

Those words have never left David.

Of course one can equate that to Elvis' psychic prowess, perhaps premonition. However, if such premonition of an early death occurred, one still wonders why he would have kept Lisa at the mansion? Others have said maybe Elvis was planning suicide. I don't buy this because of Elvis' deep religious commitments and secondly, Elvis would not have kept Lisa there if such an act were planned, and third, a suicide victim cannot take so many of their personal items to the other side, such as favorite books, clothes, jewelry . . .

I mentioned earlier in the book the name "Sivle"—Elvis

spelled backwords. Ironically there is a corporation called Sivle Enterprises Inc., listed in The Graceland Express. It is located in Florida and sells Elvis products, such as Elvis Tribute In Blue Package.

There is also a company in Japan called Orion Press, which is licensed by Presley's enterprises to produce memorabilia.

The name Orion again?

Many of the presidents of fan clubs have gone on record as saying "Vernon Presley called us personally and asked that we **not** attend the viewing nor funeral. . . ."

Maria Columbus and Jeannie Tessum, co-presidents of THE ELVIS SPECIAL, related this to me. "Vernon called us personally," Maria said. "He said it would be too hard on us. We now believe it was because Vernon knew we would **know** the truth—that it was **not** Elvis in the coffin. Vernon called a lot of other fans who knew Elvis also, asking them to stay away . . ."

This story has been supported by Bill Burk, a renowned journalist and friend of Elvis, author of THROUGH MY EYES and president of ELVIS WORLD. Others such as Elvis' longtime secretary Becky Yancey did not attend. Mae Axton, co-author of HEARTBREAK HOTEL, did not attend.

The list goes on and on.

Maria Columbus also reports something else very strange: "Not long after Elvis 'died' I received a call from him—at least I believe it was him. He called me at work. Elvis always pronounced my name Maria as 'Marear'. That's how he addressed me. I was in shock. Basically he said he was fine, not to worry . . ."

This, of course, is not the only report of Elvis contacting people after August 16, 1977, as reported earlier in this book.

(Note: on the tape authenticated as being Elvis, I noted that Elvis also pronounced the word "idea" as "idear".)

In a 1979 issue of THE ELVIS SPECIAL, Maria and Jeannie received a message from a friend . . . the author of the letter only used the initials. "J.B."

(Jon/John Burrows?)

Here is what the friend wrote. You be the judge.

206

Before I left my thoughts were of all of you. I wanted to leave behind beautiful memories for all of you to share. You see, I knew you loved me and you would grieve deeply for me. I wanted you to remember me with smiles and love . . . of a favorite song, concert or dreams. Also of my belief in my fellow men . . . always wanting the best for my family, friends and fans. Wanting to share my dreams, goals and ideas with people I love.

Now when I should be at peace and you should be going onward and growing, I feel so much hate, envy and jealousy . . . instead of leaving beautiful thoughts behind me. I find only rubbish going down as guidelines from *friends* wanting the public to know the truth of the legend known as Elvis Presley.

Just what is truth my friends—
Is *truth* calculated as *money*??
Is truth known in *friendship*??
Is truth known in *love*??
Is truth known in *caring*??
Just what is it? I need to know!

I want you to know I gave all of these in loving moments in time. I shared myself and found out that I shared it with Judas.

Friends that would turn against me after death who did not have the *courage* to face me in life. This is a reason for dying!!

Thank you Dee, Rick, David, Red, Sonny, David, Lamar and all the others to follow. Thank you for letting the *Truth* come out since I am not allowed to contribute to the great array of intelligent blood-letting. But, may I ask one question? If this is the truth what must your lies be??

I've always been hungry for love and affection. I thought *my* friends could help, but I found out that *my friends* and certain (ex) relatives only wanted two things . . . money and fame. Well folks you got it.

I wish you many, many years of love and enjoyment from life. But I have to say that you will have these *truths* on your conscience. Perhaps in a later life you can work off the Karma for putting the fans who love me through Hell. I'll pay for any Karma I have performed. You are lucky—you have time.

I send love and healing to all the people that love me.
Thank you for believing in me.

The fans had a better grip on Elvis Presley than most people have on their closest friends. They knew so much about him. Many have told me that Elvis left so many clues—that if one would stop and examine the lyrics of his last songs and **really listen** much is there. For instance Elvis changed the lyrics of WAY DOWN from "fate is growing closer, and look at my resistance, found lying on the floor" to "Fate is growing closer. Look at my resistance, found lying on the floor, *taking me to places that I've never been before* . . ." (Elvis reportedly made such changes only months pre August 1977. Recall, that Elvis was found lying on the bathroom floor. Besides adding Adios to MY WAY, there are other songs which the fans think were chosen deliberately for their "I am leaving" message.)

I related the Mike Joseph pictures, pictures which have since been shown on TV shows such as LARRY KING LIVE, OPRAH WINFREY, PEOPLE ARE TALKING/ Philadelphia, WXYZ-TV/Detroit, EVENING MAGAZINE, and originally on KCOP-TV, Los Angeles. What is interesting is that once these pictures were made public the glass door to the poolhouse has been torn down and a solid one put in its place.

As I mentioned, daily I receive new information. To date people have come forward and said they have actually seen Elvis Presley, some in Michigan, some in Hawaii, some in Memphis, all **after** August 16, 1977. Some months ago I was contacted by a radio station in Hawaii. They said that for years now they have heard from the locals about seeing Elvis Presley. They took it as useless rumors but since the tape has been known to exist, they are now asking questions. If you recall on the tape Elvis talks about Hawaii and an island he learned about "a long time ago." He went there for a year to get his health back. I have been told that there are two small islands, one owned by the military and the other by the Hawaiians, islands outside the main chain. "You have to be Hawaiian or special to the Hawaiians to reside there. Elvis was dearly loved by the Hawaiians and was made an honorary Hawaiian—he did tributes, raised money, made movies there, did his satellite there. You can be certain he would have been welcomed and given refuge . . .''

While on one of my favorite radio talk shows, KISS-FM in Columbus, Georgia, with host Bear O'Brian recently, a woman called in and identified herself. She was happy someone was brave enough to talk about this openly and to risk ridicule. She said she was afraid to tell this story for fear of such ridicule. Basically she and her husband went to Memphis last summer, arriving around 4 A.M. Driving past Graceland they decided to stop. No one was there. It was dark and silent. Simultaneously a long black sleek car pulled into the gates. There was a driver and a passenger. The windows were down. As they emerged from their own cars they looked at the passenger. ''My husband and I looked straight into the face of Elvis Presley! We were shocked. He, too, was momentarily shocked, shocked to see anyone there at that time of the morning. Suddenly the electric windows silently went up and the car proceeded through the gates and up the drive toward Graceland. No one believes what we saw. It **was** Elvis Presley.''

(Her story is on tape at the radio station for verification.)

More and more of these stories come to light via radio and television call-ins. People are now giving their names. On this same radio show another caller told of being with a well-known singer at the viewing. The singer refused to go in but the woman did. When she came back she said, ''That wasn't Elvis up there, was it?'', to which the singer replied, ''I am not at liberty to say . . .'' (Both the woman and the singer's identity are on tape at KISS in Columbus.)

On May 25, 1988 I was a guest of WXYZ-TV, an ABC affilliate in Detroit, Michigan on a show Kelley and Company. During a live interview in front of an audience John Kelley and I were interrupted by producers, directors, and station associates. One station associates. ''Elvis Presley has just called our station,'' were the words that shocked us.

Danny Jacobson, a station associate, had received a telephone call. ''The voice was shockingly familiar,'' she said. ''I felt myself go numb and I began to shake. **That voice** . . . I asked who was calling. There was a pause. 'This is Elvis Presley. I don't mean to upset you. But I want you to listen to

what is being said. It was the pressure of the business . . ."
Danny had in the meantime silently summoned over producers,
directors until there were four people listening in. They all
said it was Elvis, sounded like Elvis, had some undefinable
quality. "He wasn't nervous, like an imitator would be. I
don't know. I was shaking. That's how powerful he was . . ."
Danny said **the voice** stated he would be making an announcement soon. She also asked him about Kalamazoo,
Michigan, where Elvis had been spotted. He said he liked
Kalamazoo. This truth is confirmed by the fact Elvis often
performed there, including his last year concert tours. It
seemed an unlikely place and the population is small. Yet
everyone I've talked to who knew/knows Elvis said he did
indeed love Kalamazoo. And since Kalamazoo is only a few
hundred miles from Detroit, there could be something to this.
What is apparent though is that a very large ABC affilliate is
now questioning whether Elvis called them. Actually, they
have gone one step further. John Kelley then stood and made
an announcement to this effect: "Elvis Presley has just called
our station . . ." He then read the message.

The audience was stilled. There was a feeling in the air one
cannot describe. Suddenly the audience burst forth in ap-
plause, looked into the camera and said, "Elvis we love you.
Come back . . ."

Speaking of another television show. I recently did LARRY
KING LIVE. Since the premise of my book is not to state
Elvis is alive but rather to ask questions based on documenta-
tion together with insisting that the interviewer at least peruse
the material: listen to the authenticated tape, watch the video
and read the documented IS ELVIS ALIVE? book. I was told
Larry had done this, and was shocked to discover he had not.
That left me very vulnerable and I felt somewhat slaughtered.
However, since that show Larry is reading the material and
I've been told is very impressed and has invited me back.
During the show when Larry took call-ins a man identifying
himself as Marty Lacker, friend of Elvis and one of Elvis'
best men at Elvis' wedding, really came after me. He accused
me of exploitation (he also wrote a book) and other things.
He left the viewing audience with the impression that he had
seen the body in the coffin and Elvis **was** dead. Not being
able to determine a face via the telephone or if it was indeed

Marty Lacker, I held back. However, I have since been told by Bill Burk and Mae Axton that it was Marty's voice. So? How strange Marty would leave this impression when on page 197 of his own book PORTRAIT OF A FRIEND, Marty Lacker says in his own words that **he had not attended either the viewing nor the funeral!** I have been told that Vernon asked him not to attend.

This sort of double-talk has repeated itself often. Years ago many of the friends said one thing via media and books, from their own mouths, and now tell a totally different story. Why? Do they know something now they didn't originally know?

Marty also talks about Elvis' will, how strange it was, how pushed through it was, how Elvis disinherited just about everyone.

Truly, the hardest part about doing such a book is the subject matter. If I were talking about anyone else other than Elvis Presley the evidence would overwhelmingly point to a cover-up and even a death-hoax. After all, we have a tape, documents, pictures, sightings . . . yet just because I (and others in the media I might add) question the death of Elvis Presley we are often mocked. This again happened on THE OPRAH WINFREY SHOW. Again, even after I insist the material be perused pre-interview, this is often not done. It befuddles me as to why? I was a radio talk show hostess years ago and I made it a point to do my homework. Of course I realize Larry and Oprah have a heavy workload doing a TV show daily. In fact Larry in his marvelous book TELL IT TO THE KING makes a point of saying he doesn't read author's books. But in this case since there is an authenticated tape and a video, it would have been a wise move.

Oh well . . .

Wonderfully this has been balanced by the fantastic radio interviewers, my favorite form of media. With just one exception they have all done their homework. Paul Gonzales of WSB in Atlanta has gone far beyond the call of duty as has Bear O'Brian and Tony Thomas of KQWC in Webster City, Iowa. Both Tony and Bear have done some investigation on their own and know what I've been through. They definitely believe there might be something to the Kalamazoo sightings. They called a number given of where a John Burrows was. At first Tony was told John Burrows was in a meeting, or busy. Tony even received a call back. Finally he was told there was no John Burrows at said number, but was then asked, "What do you want with him anyway?"

Originally I never mentioned Kalamazoo but since the first edition people have come forth, some even ridiculed as they feared. Even Oprah Winfrey was in a mocking mood when some called in to her show, although now she too is taking a second look and has personally invited me back for a full hour. She is a lovely, lovely lady and I certainly understand her initial skepticism. Had she perused the tape, the video and the documentation that would have been eliminated to a great extent. Once she saw the Mike Joseph picture she appeared somewhat shocked, as is everyone.

Because it was so hard to initially get beyond the rag-mag hump, I feared those magazines would be the only ones to zero in on this. I was correct to a degree. A supermarket tabloid WEEKLY WORLD NEWS did such a story without having interviewed me. They had an artist's conception of what Elvis might look like now: bearded and balding, looking like Howard Hughes trying to be like Elvis Presley! They certainly did not get that from my book, nor did they get the Kalamazoo sightings. What is even more distressing is that the June 6th issue of NEWSWEEK ran a story using as their source of information this tabloid! In the NEWSWEEK story they told a complete lie saying I said Elvis was bald and bearding, saying I **hired** L.H. Williams, the voice ID expert. The truth is Mr. Williams is with a law enforcement agency and did this on his own time, without compensation, as did our second expert, Don Moran. NEWSWEEK also quoted a Mr. Bill De Night as saying that rather than my being a journalist I am an "Elvis Wacko." I am a published writer and journalist and not even an Elvis fan. I have never met Mr. De Night nor to my knowledge he me. I have since contacted the Editor-in-Chief of NEWSWEEK, Richard M. Smith, sending him the entire packet. I have faith he will respond with truth.

Thus you can see why I continually feel a "David" in the shadow of a mighty "Goliath."

*   *   *

Because of a world news conference at the ABA in Anaheim recently, I was allowed to present to the press a portion of the video, some of the tape and a portion of the documentation. The reaction was very positive. Everyone I talked to personally afterwards did indeed believe I had more than enough evidence to raise the question: IS ELVIS ALIVE?

Because of that person-to-person conference USA TODAY ran a front page in their LIFESTYLE section. I understand the BOSTON GLOBE, an L.A. paper, a Miami paper and others have now done very positive stories, or at least are taking a look at what I have rather than shooting off the cuff without doing any research whatsoever. These stories have been better, some excellent.

On June 1st I received a call from WABC Radio in New York. The interviewer started right off by misstating my premise. When I tried to correct him he became very angry. I remained calm and said what I've always said: I am a journalist asking questions based on documentation. When he became even more abusive I asked him if he had read the book? He told me he had no intention of ever reading such a book—no way! I then asked him if he had listened to the tape. This really blew him. "I am the interviewer," he shouted, "and if you ask me one more question I'll hang up on you!"

Calmly I reasked an essential question: "Have you listened to the tape?" There was a pause. I then asked to whom was I speaking to which he shouted that he didn't have to tell me. He then hung up on me!

Of course by now I assumed this was a crank call. No one in radio or television with an interviewer's job would behave so publically abhorrent and still keep their jobs. I had been on nearly hundred radio and television talk shows and never had this happened. The telephone rang again and this time it was Roy Fredricks, the producer I believe. He asked what happened and I suggested he replay the show. He then explained that it was Bob Grant who was doing the interview and that he had no packet. Of course that does not excuse such behaviour. I've done a few shows where the radio interviewer did not have the required packet but at least the interviewer approached it with an open ear. Never once have I had an interviewer say he had no intentions to ever, ever even study

213

the material! I would have hated to have been the one to approach a Bob-Grant type personality with the news that the world wasn't flat!

Still, I have sent WABC a packet.

The fans mean much to me. For the most part they are marvelous, warm and loving. I can understand why they are so precious to Elvis Presley. Ever since the LEGEND BOOKS editions (ORION and the book's book and tape) have been released I have received hundreds and hundreds of fan letters. 100% of the letters say they have been asking these questions publically and privately for years. Many of their own publications publically ask these questions. They even go a step further and say they believe Elvis is alive. I never say that nor have said that. I am just reporting what others say. The fans also applaud the novel ORION and its sensitivity. The people who write offer more information, more contradictions to what occurred. And as the questions keep coming, I will keep responding. There has to be answers somewhere.

On the negative side of this a fan with a newsletter has just urged RCA to prosecute me to the fullest. For what? For asking questions which have long been asked? This fan also made a false statement: she said that the tape in question was analyzed by RCA and said to be a hoax, that it was spliced together from past interviews. We had the tape checked by two top experts and it was not spliced. We then checked with the man this lady quoted at RCA and he denied ever saying such a thing! In fact he stated that his official quote was, "**Publically**, we say that Elvis Presley died 11 years ago . . ."

He asked that we send this fan's newsletter to him, which we are doing. He can take it from there. We may also take action against her and ask her to present official documentation on the tape to the contrary.

Sound like a shoot-off at the O.K. corral?

I also just learned but have not read it, that a newspaper in Florida has stated that Graceland is suing me. Not true. Again, to be sued for asking questions based on documentation is nonsense. Is Graceland going to sue each and every fan who has publically asked such questions, some via sold-for newsletters? Are they going to go after ABC? Are they going to go after those people who have publically claimed to have seen Elvis? How many magazines, tabloids, radio and television shows could they handle?

Did Graceland sue 20/20? No, in fact it was the reverse. 20/20 initiated a lawsuit trying to gain records.

There are too many questions. I would like someone to explain the tape, the Mike Joseph pictures, the sightings. If I find out the answers I'll happily relate them, no matter what. In fact a phoney tape has been presented. I had it voice authenticated. It was not Elvis Presley.

What happened to me with the novel ORION happened. It in itself is bizarre. My publicist at LEGENDS received a telephone call while I was on WSB with Paul Gonzales. "Tell Gail," the mystery voice stated, "that the matter concerning the cover-up is more far reaching and involves more power and money than she even realizes. What she has discovered is only the tip of the iceberg . . ."

AFTERMATH

When I finally received my ORION reprint rights back from Simon and Schuster/Pocket Books, I was advised by a top New York literary agent to write a book-about-the-book.

Part of the advice focused on the problem of getting the novel ORION back out. "I am afraid that prospective publishers will view Orion as simply a reprint sale, when in truth the novel never had a chance. They would check with S&S and find out that it had a short sales cycle without ever knowing the true story. It's a wonderful, exciting book and it deserves it's 'day in the sun.' "

Because the story behind the novel was so involved, it would have been impossible to tell in a brief conversation and might end up sounding like a misplaced lament. But to do the book-about-the-book again placed me in a Catch-22 situation: in order for me to sell ORION, I would have to allow personal correspondence to be viewed and thus cross over into the literary professional bedmate theory.

I have pointed out some very strange occurrences, coincidences and relationships connected with the demise of ORION. I am coming from the perspective of a victim. Still, I make no accusations, but rather ask the type of questions that seem reasonable under the circumstances.

I do not know what will happen, not with ORION, not with the many questions posed concerning Elvis and his "death."

Ironically, just as it appears that the end may not have occurred for Elvis Presley on August 16, 1977, it also appears this particular book does not end here.

A FINAL NOTE . . .

Around the 10th anniversary of the death of Elvis Presley, an Atlanta attorney, who had been working in the Gary Hart campaign, responded to the rumor that Gary Hart would run again with this statement: "The probability of Gary Hart seeking the nomination for President of the United States is as unlikely a possibility as believing Elvis Presley is still alive."

Less than four months after this statement, on December 15, 1987, Gary Hart again announced his candidacy for President of the United States.

ACKNOWLEDGMENTS

My deepest appreciation to Mae Axton. To Cindy, Jay, Murray and Edith Baum, To S.C. of Cub Run, Cohen Davis, P.S.D., David and Rose Dortort, Avrum Fine, Marilou Schuster, Norman Shavin, Mitch and Dianne Slayton, Renice Strain, Elizabeth Pierce, Debby Thompson, and Louise Welling.

Thanks to Dick Sutter for his marketing expertise.

Thanks to editor Gale Crudup, and to assistants Carolyn Duncan and M.B. Danielski.

Heartfelt thanks to L.H. Williams for voice print work.

Thanks to Carole Halupke for permission to print lyrics to her songs ORION and MY BROTHER MY TWIN.

A very special thanks to Maria Columbus, co-president of THE ELVIS SPECIAL, in Pacifica, California. Maria provided me with support and material.

An extra hug to TOM BOWEN BREWER.

A number of previously published books about Elvis were consulted, occasionally for direct quotations or information, more often for confirmation. They include:

ELVIS, by Albert Goldman, McGraw-Hill, New York

ELVIS: WHAT HAPPENED? by Red West, Sonny West and Dave Hebler as told to Steve Dunleavy, Ballantine Books, New York

ELVIS AND GLADYS by Elaine Dundy, Macmillan Publishing, New York

ELVIS: WE LOVE YOU TENDER by Dee Presley, Billy, Rick and David Stanley as told to Martin Torgoff, Dell Publishing Co., Inc., New York

ELVIS THE FINAL YEARS by Jerry Hopkins, St. Martins Press, Inc., New York

ARE YOU LONESOME TONIGHT? by Lucy de Barbin and Dary Matera, Villard Books—Random House, New York

ELVIS AND ME by Priscilla Beaulieu Presley with Sandra Harmon, G. P. Putnum's, New York

THE ELVIS CATALOG by Lee Cotten

ELVIS by Dave Marsh, New York Times Books, New York

ELVIS AFTER LIFE by Dr. Raymond Moody, Peachtree Publishers, Atlanta, Georgia.

ELVIS . . . WHERE ARE YOU? by Steven Chanzes, Direct Products, Inc., Florida

ELVIS IN PRIVATE by Peter Haining, St. Martins Press, New York

To KCOP in Los Angeles for quoting from their program of January 8, 1986.

From ABC's 20/20 with Geraldo Rivera on THE COVER-UP IN THE DEATH OF ELVIS PRESLEY—1979

PHOTOSCREEN Magazine
PEOPLE Magazine
US MAGAZINE
PLAYBOY MAGAZINE

THE ELVIS SPECIAL fan newsletters
ROUSTABOUT fan newsletters

James Bacon, LOS ANGELES HERALD
Bob Greene, CHICAGO TRIBUNE
Ken Lefolii, THE WINDSOR STAR, Toronto, Canada

There is more to this incredible story . . .

The book that Gail Brewer-Giorgio imagined and then, incredibly, seemed only too true . . .

ORION

THE NOVEL

by Gail Brewer-Giorgio

Coming this fall in paperback from Tudor Publishing.